TROKOSI

"SLAVE OF THE GODS"

Linda M. Gillard *(white author)*

Modern day stories of women and children who have lived horrific lives as slaves. Even now in the 21st century, it is estimated that there are over 30,000 trokosis living in West Africa who are given away by their families, as little virgin girls, to atone for a crime that they didn't even commit. They are forced to live in shrines shrouded by secrecy, and are bound by forces that control their lives, without the hope of ever being liberated.

Xulon PRESS

TROKOSI
by Linda M. Gillard

Printed in the United States of America

ISBN 9781615798513

Any Bible Scripture quoted in this book has been taken from Today's New International Version. Copyright © 2006 by Zondervan, Grand Rapids, MI. USA

The photograph on the front cover is of three trokosis waiting to be liberated at a ceremony that will be performed by the two fetish priests sitting next to them.

gillardquilting@msn.com

www.xulonpress.com

This book is dedicated to my family, friends, and church, who encouraged me in my quest to visit the Republic of Ghana in West Africa, in search of some answers regarding the brutal, ancient cultural practice of trokosi, which is still shrouded in secrecy even today.

Thank you so much for all your prayers and support along the way. This book was made possible because of you.

The following information and stories were compiled by the author and was written from the author's perspective, by the experiences gained while visiting the Republic of Ghana, the Adidome Training Centre run by International Needs Network and the Ewe people of the Volta region. It is a personal portrayal of what was seen, heard and discussed by those who chose to share with the author, as well as information that was "found" by other honest means. The author does not claim to understand all of the cultural practices of the Ghanaian people, but found the Ghanaian people in general to be a friendly, honest, hard working people of honour, with hope for a better future.

*Our lives begin to end
the day we become silent
about things that matter.*

Martin Luther King

Trokosi – slave of the gods

There's no one to care for me, here
at the shrine
I'm alone and I'm frightened 'cause
I'm only nine.

I'm hungry and tired, but I cannot rest.
There is work to be done and I do try my best,

But the beatings continue at the hands
of the priest.
The load is too heavy; still I work like a beast.

I'm paying atonement for another man's sin.
I will live my whole life with the
fear that's within.

The gods have demanded a small virgin child,
And I am the chosen one, unloved and beguiled.

I'm afraid when I'm sleeping, as I am of use
To the fetish priest's lust, and his sexual abuse.

So who then will love me and dry up my tears,
And hold me so tightly, to push away fears.

Please open your heart, reach into your purse,
To love me and free me from this awful curse.

Linda Gillard

Table of Contents

Chapter 1

Charity's Story

The practice of trokosi, which means, "slave of the gods" or "wife of the gods" in West Africa, was something I had never heard of up until a year or so ago. In the Ewe language, "tro" means deity or fetish, and "kosi" means female slave. Needless to say, I was horrified as I researched and discovered what the practice of trokosi actually detailed, and then to find out that this practice still exists today in some countries where children pay dearly for the crimes, offences, or sins of others.

Little virgin girls are given to the shrines and serve as slaves in ritualistic sexual bondage to the fetish priests, some as young as 3 years old. These innocent children are given to the shrines by their parents under fear of death curses, that are carried out by the fetish priests of the local villages where idol worship takes place inside the shrines. Most of these parents do not want to give up their children, and many are heartbroken when the gods choose their child, but they fear the power of the voodoo practices and curses of the fetish (or voodoo) priests (commonly known as "witchdoctors" many years ago) and so, because of fear, they feel they have no other choice than to allow their children to be sent to the shrine as trokosis. From my understanding the practice of voodoo originated in the country of Ghana, and it is still practiced today within the fetish shrines.

If a crime has been committed in a village, the fetish priest is called in to deal with the issue at hand. At any time the crime, sin, or transgression can be real or imagined, petty or enormous. Sometimes it is the grandfather of the little girl chosen to become a trokosi, who has had an affair with another woman, and at other times it could be a cousin who is the alleged thief, and so on. The offender is not the one who is punished, but a virgin girl in the criminal's family pays an enormous price for the crime. The offended person would take their grievances to the fetish priest and ask to have a curse put on the family of the perpetrator. The offending family is cursed through a ritual that is conducted by the fetish priest causing mysterious illnesses, bad luck and even death to destroy various family members, therefore fear rules at this point. The "guilty" party (or the family of the convicted one) realizing that something needs to change in order to carry on in good health, etc. will go to the fetish priest and ask what needs to be done to have the curse revoked. The fetish priest will then conduct another ceremony asking the gods or deities what they desire or need to be appeased, and the gods will ask for a virgin girl to serve as a trokosi in the shrine, to atone for the sin or crime of her family member. The fetish priest is given the name of a child that the gods desire (by their gods during the ceremony) to serve in the shrine. Should the family choose not to give up the child asked for, the curse will not be lifted and family members will continue to have bad luck or die, and eventually the heartbroken parents of the little girl will agree to give her to the shrine as a slave of the gods.

We have all heard the history of Elmina castle off the coast of Ghana where slaves were brought and held until they were exported to America and other countries. More than 40 million Africans were deported over a period of about 350 years to serve as slaves. The fact that the people of Africa were "stolen" away from their families and homes was atrocious, so who would have thought that it was still happening today, in one form or another. The thing that I couldn't understand at first, was that the trokosis are equally as abused as the slaves of yesterday, but in this case they are being exploited by their own families, villages, culture and religion, and it is considered (by some) to be a privilege to serve as a slave of the gods, except by the women and children who are serving as the slaves. What's wrong with this picture?

These girls are considered "living sacrifices" and property of the fetish priests. As long as they remain in the shrine or under the control of the fetish priest, it is felt that the anger of the gods will be appeased, and no harm will come to her family for the alleged or genuine crime that was committed. A little girl is chosen by the gods (not by the fetish priest- as he is the go between) and she is put through degrading ceremonies where her clothing, jewellery and even her name is taken from her. A cloth is put between her thighs and a rope around her neck. She is then dressed in the identifying "garb" of a trokosi and can never remove the rope, or even wear a different style of clothing. The clothing of a trokosi can change from shrine to shrine, but the rope remains the same as I understand it. She is stripped of her dignity, her childhood, and her life as she knew it.

11

At times a little girl is given as a slave to the shrine to thank the gods for a child being conceived. If a person is thought to be healed, or if some other significant wonder happens, a little girl can also be given to the shrine via the fetish priest, in appreciation. In the case of a family having a lot of bad luck, they may offer a virgin girl hoping their luck will change. Other times, several generations of virgin girls are given for one particular crime or sin that was committed decades ago. All of the trokosi children serve with hard labour at the shrine on the shrine's land, which is owned by that particular village. They are not even supplied with the basic necessities of life. They are not compensated with money, food, medical help, education or even affection. They are horribly sexually, mentally, emotionally and physically abused and serve as literal slaves to the priests, elders and owners of these shrines. If a child dies from lack of food or an illness, or runs away, she is replaced by another little girl in that family, sometimes for several generations. In those cases, sometimes no one can even remember what the original crime was. If a priest tires of a particular girl he may return her and another child will take her place, but even then the other girl can be called back to the shrine at any time in her life, as she is still considered property. Sometimes three or four girls consecutively have to pay for the same petty or alleged crime. Their families must supply them with food, however, that is not usually possible because of the distance they may have to travel, or they may lack the extra food, so after toiling from before dawn 'til late in the evening, in the searing African sun, these little girls have to find other ways to feed themselves. Many times they go without food and it is not uncommon for them to be malnourished. After they have had their third menstrual cycle (and sometimes before), these girls are raped and impregnated by the fetish priests, and their children also serve as slaves alongside their mothers. There is nothing they can do about the abuse. They are owned by the gods of the shrine and the priests are allowed to do as they please. These little girls and women feel absolutely worthless in their roll as trokosis.

Many generations ago when the Ewe people were fighting in tribal wars over land issues, the idols in the shrines were obtained as gods who would kill – that was their purpose. I did hear stories that virgin girls were given to the idols and shrines to appease the gods of war, so that the enemy would die and their battle would be won. The function of some of these shrine idols is to kill. I heard from several sources that on some occasions when the gods were very angry, trokosis had been ritualistically sacrificed (murdered) in the shrines to appease the anger of the gods, but no one could give me any more information than that, because of the shroud of secrecy regarding the activity in the shrines, and I am sure that out of fear no one wanted to be involved in something as sinister as murder.

The cultural practice of trokosi (female slavery) is over 300 years old, and even though in 1998 the Ghanaian parliament passed a law banning all forms of ritualized forced labour and slavery, this custom still exists. Fear of the gods keeps government officials from actually stopping the ancient cultural practice. Since the trokosis are considered property of the shrines they are totally controlled by the fetish priests (or witch doctors of old). It is a given, in most liberal or free countries, that anyone who performs services that are not volunteered for, not paid for, and are held against their will, beaten and abused at will, are slaves or hostages. Some traditionalists claim that trokosis are not actual slaves, but that it is a privilege for them to be "chosen" to live in a shrine as a "wife" of the gods. In the shrines it is considered a duty for a trokosi who has come to the age of puberty to copulate with the priest of the shrine, as his genitalia have been blessed by the gods, and it is considered a sacred act – at least in the mind of the fetish priest. Liberated trokosis will tell you a different story. They are forced into sexual slavery, and in fact repeatedly raped by the fetish priests and sometimes even by the elders living in the village. They have no choice other than to accept what is done to them. They learn soon enough not to fight or refuse what is forced upon them, as the punishments are severe for any thing perceived as disobedience or an act of defiance. Because of fear of the god of vengeance and the demonic power of the fetish priests and the deities, they feel that they will die if they run away, as that is what they are told. They have seen the "black magic" or strong powers of their owners – the voodoo of the fetish priests. Girls who do try and escape and return back to the village of their families are forcefully returned, as there is a penalty or fine (imposed on them by the fetish priests or elders of the villages) if they help the escapee. Also, the very real fear that the curse will remain on the family, forces family members to return the child to the shrine, where they are beaten for trying to flee. For them, life is hopeless.

Many liberated trokosis have described severe beatings and other forms of punishment for refusing to co-operate with the perverted demands of their owners. Their screams are punished during the rape and their silent cries afterwards are ignored. There is no one to comfort them – ever. They are not allowed to be touched in any way by anyone except the fetish priests, and they will never show any affection to the trokosis. They cannot be hugged or treated with any tenderness, whatsoever. Should they not meet their work quota, or if they refuse the sexual advances, they are sometimes given their only "choice" in life as a trokosi, when a whip-like cane or broken chards of shells are laid out in front of them. They can choose to be held down by others, and whipped in the same fashion that a cotton-picking slave of an American plantation was whipped in the 1800's, or they can choose to kneel on the sharp broken pieces of shell for hours, with no medical help afterwards. There are other equally painful punishments dealt out for any minor offences that the fetish priest deems punishable.

Traditionalist organizations such as the Afrikania Mission (which sounds good, but isn't really a mission at all, as we know missions to be) defend their stand, claiming that the practice of trokosi is a religion or a cultural practice and should be protected. They also deny (except for the odd case) that there is any evidence of sexual ritualistic abuse (when in fact there are huge files of evidence to the contrary). They state that it is forbidden for a trokosi to be sexually active. On the other hand, International Needs workers and former trokosis who have been liberated say that they had no choice as to whether or not they would become a trokosi, and that the number of children born to them while living at the shrine bears witness to the fact that they were indeed sexually exploited and enslaved. They also say with their new life of freedom, that there is no turning back for them. It is extremely hard for the liberated trokosi to get "past" the past. Extensive counselling is needed to rehabilitate these women and children.

The fetish priests will not admit to sexually abusing the women and girls, so to date no one has ever been imprisoned for exploiting one of these children, even though the crime of "ritual or customary servitude" carries (only) a 3 year mandatory prison term in Ghana. Sometimes a priest will marry some of the girls, but one of the liberated trokosis was overheard saying that there was no benefit to being a wife of the priest, as she was still a slave and had no wifely privileges, or even any kind of affection. She was not given a choice in the marriage. She was not allowed to refuse, and one would think that since the problem of rape and sexual abuse is too well documented now to be disputed, there was no benefit whatsoever to marrying a fetish priest.

Years ago (and still to this day) there was a lot of secrecy regarding the shrines and the practises that went on within their walls and the Ewe people of Ghana were too afraid to discuss what really went on, as they feared the power of the voodoo practices, the fetish priests and the gods. Information was not widely available, but since the 1990's, International Needs, Every Child Ministries, human rights organizations, and other groups concerned about the fate of the trokosis have gotten involved, and many articles that are readily available on the internet reveal their deplorable situations. Other articles have also been written in the newspapers of Ghana. On occasion, radio and T.V. programs have also been broadcast in the USA and other countries. Still, the practice of trokosi is not well known in North America and other countries. Even in the 21st century, there is still a shroud of secrecy regarding the trokosis and the rituals of the fetish priests in the shrines of Ghana.

Apparently, in the mid eighteenth century some missionaries would "purchase" trokosis to give them their freedom and convert them to Christianity, but the idea of buying them back with money just wasn't feasible as there were too many, as well as the purchased slaves could and would be replaced by other little virgin girls. It was also highly dangerous for the missionaries involved. The liberated trokosis also needed to be educated to support themselves and their children, and that was almost impossible. Without an actual liberation ceremony that is done by the fetish priest, the curse remained on the family.

As of late, liberation is done on a shrine-by-shrine basis and when an agreement is reached, the trokosis are liberated by the fetish priests through International Needs and then given an education, a trade, counselling and extensive rehabilitation so that they are able to support themselves and their children in the future. The owners of the shrine are given compensation for releasing the women and children, and that particular shrine is banned from ever taking trokosis again. A contract is signed by all involved and the fetish priest will not go back on his word, as he must do as the gods dictate. I do know that when a shrine liberates trokosis in a village, International Needs will try to establish a school in the area of the village and if possible, even put in a well to help stop diseases brought on by contaminated water. I. N. (International Needs) befriends the fetish priests and the villagers, and will do whatever is in their power to help as needed. When the fetish priest signs the contract with I.N. Network, he will honour the agreement as he believes that if he goes against what was agreed upon, he will fall ill and die as the contract was signed in the presence (and with the consent) of the gods that he serves.

Medical teams from other countries donate their time and expertise on behalf of International Needs and travel to as many of the villages that can be reached, to administer medical attention to those in need.

The hope of all advocates of the trokosis, is that eventually all fetish priests will accept goats, cows or other animals to pay for the crimes of others instead of a virgin girl. One priest was overheard to say, "You can't have sex with a cow." Now, how is that for admitting that they do indeed sexually abuse the trokosis? Unfortunately, liberated trokosis are still sometimes shunned or ostracized because of the fear of many Ewe people. Many of these women will never be able to marry, as some people believe that trokosis who have been liberated can bring bad luck. I would imagine that some liberated trokosis would not even be interested in a man ever again, but then again, I am only imagining. Many others, I am sure would love to have a kind loving husband and family.

My understanding is that recently International Needs was asked by the officials of Benin and Togo to help liberate the voodoosis in their countries (trokosis in their language – notice the beginning of the word – voodoo), but there are never enough funds or field workers to do it all. Since beginning their work, International Needs has liberated, educated, and rehabilitated over 3,000 trokosi women and children, although it is thought that upwards toward 30,000 female slaves still exist in four different African countries.

The practice of trokosi is an evil and vile form of degrading women and children and needs to be completely annihilated. There is a fear that the practice of trokosi has gone underground in some places, as traditionalists feel that International Needs and other human rights groups are interfering with cultural practices. I will write later on about the trokosis who are enslaved on the "other side" of the Volta River and the hostility that the fetish priests (and others) have towards outsiders who want to liberate their slaves.

When one's freedom depends on another's so called "rights" as a cultural practice, things need to change drastically. One cannot keep a cultural practice when that same practice steals the dignity, freedom and God given human rights of others. When women cannot speak for themselves, others need to speak for them. Women and children need to be empowered in order to change anything in their lives. The way to empower them is through education, however, education is not free in Ghana, and unless a child is sponsored, they remain illiterate and powerless to change their situations in the villages and towns of the Republic of Ghana, or anywhere else for that matter.

Recently, I had the opportunity to visit Ghana at the invitation of International Needs to do some field work gathering information and real life stories from the liberated trokosis at the Adidome Training Centre that is run by International Needs. I spent only a couple of weeks in Ghana and don't pretend to know and understand all of their customs. I can only tell you of my experiences, thoughts and feelings while visiting their land to gather information on the culture and tradition of the trokosis, and the Ewe (pronounced Ay – vay) people of Ghana.

The following information was given to me by various Ghanaians that I spoke with, as well as by what I perceived as a Canadian visiting a foreign third world country 12,000 kilometres away from the comforts of my own home. Those two weeks will never be forgotten. I wrote insanely in a journal every night, sometimes even while sitting under my mosquito net with a flashlight while the power was out in my little guest room. I recorded everything that I felt, saw and heard, with the hope that I would somehow be able to pass on what I experienced, with some stories and a little bit of information as to the plight of the trokosis who are hidden away in a dark world of pain and endless suffering, that no woman or beast should ever have to endure. My hope is that these stories that I gathered will be the key that unlocks the hearts of others who care deeply about women and children everywhere who are in dire need of our help, as they have no resources to help themselves.

Some names and stories were changed slightly to protect some of the liberated trokosis who were fearful of being exploited. Many others had equally horrendous lives, but did not feel comfortable sharing with me as it was too painful to dig up the old memories. Some of the stories were very unemotional and mechanical, as I believe that to give any gruesome details would again have been too painful. In those cases I just got a lot of simple answers. No extra details were given to me on a voluntary basis. Other women sobbed as they told me how they suffered, living as trokosis in the shrines. Some had a hard time looking me (a stranger) in the eye while they shared, and others did not want to be identified as they may be perceived as "bad" by their own people. They loved their country, friends and families, and did not want to appear as though they were "bad-mouthing".

The following story was told to me by a liberated trokosi who had chosen the name of Charity after she turned her back on the traditional religion that brought her nothing but pain and suffering. She was baptised in the Christian faith and was happy as a Christian, as it brought hope and peace to her life. She said that there was no turning back as her traditional religion only brought heartache and sorrow to her.

My name is Charity, but that is not the name that I was given at birth. I came from a large family of nine girls and five boys. My family loved me, but we were in a traditional

Ewe religion and we were afraid of the demonic power and the deities of the fetish priest in our village. Our gods of vengeance were unspeakably evil and extremely powerful, and we were ruled by fear of what they could do, if we didn't obey. We don't keep track of birth dates in the Ewe culture, so I think that I was about seven or eight years old when I was given to the shrine as a trokosi, to be a slave of the gods.

I was not given any information, nor did I find out what was happening with the week long rituals and celebrations, that I was going through in my village. I did not find out until years later, why I had been chosen by the gods to go and live in the shrine.

The story was that my great-grandmother had been accused of stealing some gold ear rings. Apparently, someone had visited my great-grandmother and had left her gold ear rings behind by mistake. The ear rings had been put aside to give back to her, but when the person came to get them, they had disappeared. Someone had stolen them from my great-grandmother's house, but it was not known who took them.

The visitor was very angry and went to the fetish priest to have a curse put on my great-grandmother's family (that curse would cover the whole extended family) and because of the curse, my family members were falling ill and dying. The fetish priest had taken the complaint to the god of vengeance, to have a curse put on my family.

Some members of my family went to the fetish priest to see how the gods could be appeased so that the curse would be lifted, and after the fetish priest again invoked the gods, my family was told that the gods demanded a young virgin girl to atone for the stolen gold ear rings. I was the girl that was chosen (and named) by the god of vengeance, and no one else could take my place in order to have the curse reversed. Even though I was an innocent child, I was the one who had to pay for the rest of my life, for the alleged crime of the stolen ear rings. I also found out that I was a replacement trokosi as another little girl from my village had been chosen as a slave for that crime, but she had died while at the shrine, so I had to take her place and atone for the sin of another. I understand now why it didn't matter if we were fed or taken care of while we lived at the shrine. It didn't matter if we died, as we could easily be replaced by another small virgin girl. We were of no value as individuals.

During the rituals and ceremonies, all of my clothes were taken off me and I was stripped of my birth name forever. My jewellery was taken and I was to own nothing but the calico (white cotton) wrap that was put on me (which covers from the chest down). Around my neck a twisted or braided rope was put, and I was told that I could not take it off. It was identical to the rope that the fetish priest wears around his neck. I was now wearing the garb that a trokosi wore for identification, but I was still not aware of what was happening. No one shared anything with me and I was too young to figure things out for myself. Everything was so secretive. I didn't understand what was happening to me or why I was going through the ceremonies. I think they knew that if they had told me in advance as to what was happening, that I would have tried to run away. One ceremony went from the top of my head right to my feet, as they were presenting me to the shrine as a "wife" or "slave" of the gods of that shrine. I was washed in holy water to make me acceptable to the gods (or the idols that represented the gods) of the shrine.

My mother and father walked along with me, as well as some of the elders on the way to the village where the shrine was, without telling me anything. I was not afraid, as my parents were with me. Once we got to the shrine, there was another celebration the next day, and then my parents left me there. I was told that I was not to go home with them. It was then that I realized that my parents had already left, and I was alone. I started to cry, but was told that I was never allowed to cry again, or I would be beaten with a cane - a thin stick that is more like a whip. I didn't understand why they would leave me alone with no family, in a strange village to live in the shrine when I was such a small child. I felt so unloved, rejected and alone. I had been abandoned to total strangers who didn't even care that I was there. I was heartbroken. I was told that I could never wear regular clothing again, but must wear the rope and calico the rest of my life to be identified as a trokosi.

There were about sixty trokosis living in that shrine and we all lived together and slept in that crowded mud shrine. I would not be allowed to visit with the villagers, as now I was a slave. I was not allowed to play with the other children, as a curse could rub off on them. Also, I had been cleansed and made holy for the gods to use, and I could be contaminated by others if they touched me in any way. I was so little that one of the older slaves taught me how to cook for myself and how to learn some basic survival skills. After that, I was on my own. No one cared for me. No one was allowed to show me any tenderness or love. Affection wasn't allowed. Happiness or joy wasn't allowed, besides there was nothing to be joyful or happy about. Everything about our lives as trokosis was all about fear, sadness, pain, and misery.

We were all in the same position - hungry and tired, sick and unhappy, abused and unloved. I was responsible for taking care of myself, and if I wanted to eat, I had to figure out how that would be done. We had to get up very early before dawn and head out to the fields to work. Unlike the other villagers who would finish work around noon when the sun was too hot, we had to continue working until it was dark. For a little child, it was unbearable at times. The loads were just too hard for me, and I would get beaten mercilessly with a cane for any infraction. I would get beaten any time the fetish priest was displeased with anything I had done. Sometimes I was beaten for seemingly nothing.

If there was a good crop we would be allowed to eat from it, but most of the time we were suffering from such hunger. We were so malnourished that we suffered with diseases and illness much of the time, but were still expected to work hard. I would cry and get beaten mercilessly with a cane, so I learned to find a place to hide if I had to cry and then I would wipe my face and eyes, so that no one would know that I had been crying. If we were too sick or hungry to work, we would get beaten severely. If we didn't work hard enough we were also beaten. The abuse was terrible.

My birth name had been taken from me at the initial ceremony and I was given the name of, "Gold Ear Rings." All of the trokosis at our shrine were named after the crimes that they were atoning for. I was told that I would be there forever and would die there while paying for the alleged crime of my great-grandmother. By that time, I was aware of why I was serving as a slave of the gods, but I didn't know why "I" specifically had been chosen by the deities to pay for someone else's sin. I will never know.

My mother came to visit me only once while I was there. I was never able to see my family again while I was a trokosi. I don't know if it was too painful for my mother to visit me, or if she just wasn't allowed. Families were allowed to bring food for their own enslaved children, but most people had to travel too far, or there just wasn't enough food for them. I lived a life of such depravation. I knew that the abuse would never end. I was an innocent child and was treated so brutally.

One day, when I was about ten or eleven years old, the priest asked someone to tell me to go somewhere, for one reason or another. The fetish priest had lust on his mind and he followed me to where I was told to go. When he got me alone, he forced himself on me and raped me. He didn't tell me what he was going to do, or even talk to me. I didn't understand what he was doing. He just took what he wanted without considering what that rape did to me. It was so terrifying! I was worse off than a dog. There was nothing that I could do about the sexual abuse. I was a slave of the gods and the fetish priest had the right to rape me whenever he wanted. To refuse the sexual advances of the fetish priest would make him angry and I would be beaten ruthlessly. The sexual abuse was the worst thing about being a trokosi. Every day I was always afraid. The gods we served were not gods of love and kindness. The fruits that they delivered were pain, torture and even murder. I had four children by the fetish priest and had to feed and care for them as well as myself, and still had to work hard in the fields every day. My children had to come with me to the fields, as it was my responsibility to see that they learned to work hard to keep them from being beaten as well. Life was very hard for all of us living at the shrine. I have no good memories as a trokosi – none.

About ten years ago, International Needs came to our village, and although it took quite some time, they came to an agreement with the fetish priest and elders of the village, and because of that contract we found out that we were going to be liberated. We didn't find this out until the agreement had been reached. No one told us anything. It was all a very big surprise when we found out, as we never had any hope of ever being liberated. We had to have a liberation ceremony performed by the fetish priest, so that the gods would be satisfied, thus insuring that we would no longer have to atone for the sins of a family member. Our families needed to know that the curse would be lifted before we could go back to our villages, because of the fear of the gods that everyone lived with. The gods were powerful and the curses were very real. If the fetish priest did not do a liberation ceremony, no one in our own villages would have let us come back.

Once we were liberated, we went to the Adidome Training Centre to learn trades and various skills so that we could support our children. I received counselling along with rehabilitation for two years, and I learned how to pray. I sought the true and living, good and kind God that I was learning about, and I found him. I decided to become a Christian and serve Jesus and was baptised and took the name of Charity. I now work at the Adidome Training Centre as one of the cooks for the students. I help prepare the meals. I live in the next village and my children are going to school and getting an education.

My hope is that my children get a good education and that they are able to have a better lifestyle.

After my interview with Charity, I felt rather sad and disturbed. I had a difficult time asking her questions, as I realized that I was digging up old wounds. I had never been face to face with someone who had such a horrific story to tell. I noticed that when I watched her working at the compound, there was a kind of sadness about her. She was a very beautiful woman and would smile a sad smile, when she saw me (I think out of courtesy), but she always seemed to be deep in thought. I did hear from someone that Charity had fallen in love with a man a few years earlier, but when she told him that she was a liberated trokosi, she never saw him again. I have no other details. I am sure she thought about the wasted years that she had endured with her children, and thought if only she could have turned back the clock. I think that maybe the man she loved must have still believed in the old way, and thought that perhaps Charity still carried a curse and wanted no part of that. I wanted to feel her pain as I did feel so sad about her little girl memories and the horrible life she had lived as a former trokosi. She was as happy as she could be with what she had and she did have hope for the future of her children. At one point, after interviewing many liberated trokosis, I told the translator that I didn't think I could listen to another horrific story and that I figured I had enough information; however there was another story that I needed to hear that had a good ending. I will get to that later on.

Chapter 2

My Arrival

I arrived in Ghana at 8:00 P.M. local time, which was two in the morning at home. It was refreshing to step out of the aircraft into a gentle warm breeze and 25 degrees C. A few days earlier it had been minus 48 C. in Saskatchewan, and I was looking forward to some sunny warm weather. Little did I know that I would long for the snow and home, before my two week stay in Ghana was over.

I was blessed to have Pastor Larry and my church family pray for me in the Sunday morning service before I left for the airport that afternoon. How wonderful it felt to have so many people supporting me on this trip. I was touched by their kindness and generosity.

The first leg of my journey was quite uneventful. It was only two hours to Minneapolis from Regina and after a two hour wait I was on the next flight to Amsterdam, which took almost nine hours. I had not been able to take time for breakfast or lunch that Sunday morning and I was carrying a back pack full of snacks – just in case. I was also loaded *down with hundreds of little metal cars to give to the African children that I was hoping to meet.*

An hour after we lifted off for Amsterdam. I assumed that we weren't getting a meal on this flight either, so decided to break out the cheese and crackers, as well as a small "pop open" can of salmon. I wolfed it down quickly, only to discover that the salmon and my stomach were having an awful battle. Fortunately, the bathroom was vacant and I "hurled" all that I had inhaled. No sooner had I reclaimed my seat, I noticed a wonderful smell of chicken coming from across the aisle. We were being served a full course chicken dinner after all, and I was too nauseous to eat. I asked for some ginger ale to wash down a couple of acid reflux pills in hopes of settling my stomach and I had to pass on the chicken dinner.

Since we were travelling at night, I took out my newly purchased travel pillow, inflated it and proceeded to try and get some "shut eye." I was fortunate enough to have a vacant seat beside me, so thought I would curl up into a ball and get some sleep. I sure wanted to stretch out as I did in our king sized bed at home. The inexpensive travel pillow had rough edges on it that poked into my neck no matter what angle I repositioned it to. At the best of times I am an insomniac, and usually take something to make me relax enough to get to sleep, but I didn't want to arrive in Amsterdam at three in the morning and have to be forcefully dragged off of the aircraft due to the effects of a "Gravol" or some other pharmaceutical. I thought that may cause more problems than it was worth, so I opted to go without a sleep aid and ended up with no sleep at all, and a stiff neck to boot! That was only the first half of my journey.

After another gruelling 8 hour flight from Amsterdam to Accra, I arrived. The one thing that I did enjoy immensely was viewing the sand dunes in the desert below, from the aircraft window. It was so fascinating to see the shadows on the desert from the dunes. I wondered how tall they must have been, in order to be able to see them from such a high altitude.

After quite a lengthy line up going through customs, I managed to locate my entire incredibly heavy luggage set. As I dragged my two 70 pound suitcases along, I prayed that their puny little wheels wouldn't give out before my "ride" arrived. My back pack which had at least 20 pounds of AA batteries, along with another 20 pounds of "stuff" was ripping my shoulders back so that when I caught a glimpse of myself in a window; it appeared as though I was walking up hill. I tried to the best of my abilities to straighten up and look more relaxed, but it wasn't easy. As well, I had my heavy camera bag bobbing around in front of me in such a manner that it was chafing my neck. I was trying to even out the load that I was carrying.

As I arrived at the security check point, I was required to open up my bags once again for a final fifth or sixth check, after which I carefully loaded up my person once again, without trying to appear as though I was under too much stress due to the excess weight I was hauling. It was quite interesting that I was never charged anything extra for the oversized loads that I took with me, but I wasn't going to draw that to anyone's attention either.

Being in an airport in a foreign land, that I wasn't accustomed to, I had a hard time trying to figure out where everyone was supposed to be met by their friends or families. Except for passengers, I didn't see anyone who looked like they were waiting for the expected passengers. I didn't want to appear too old or stupid (my kids sometimes made me feel that way) so I sure wasn't going to ask anyone any stupid questions – not yet anyway. I was getting a little nervous, as I didn't see anyone waiting for me inside the terminal, but then there didn't seem to be anyone waiting for others either. For a moment I thought that I had perhaps been forgotten about, until I was directed (with the other passengers) outside to a massive crowd lined up outside of a fenced off area. It was already dark out, and it didn't help much when I didn't know who I was looking for. Slowly, I trudged along with my excessively heavy baggage, hoping that I would figure out who in this massive collection of dark faces was there to pick me up, when all of a sudden I spotted my name on a large white card which was being held by a friendly looking fellow with a smiling face. I was relieved to say the least, and walked in the direction of the card.

Fred was one of the International Needs Network (I.N.) staff who had been sent to take me to a hotel for the night, as it was too late to head out to the Adidome Training Centre that evening. We drove along for some time winding through this lane and that while making some small talk. They tried to make me feel comfortable as I didn't have a clue what to say to the two gentlemen with me.

I was taken to a small old hotel that had been recently renovated. It was quite quaint and it was more than adequate. The bell hops cheerfully took my luggage and one of them hoisted one of my 70 pound suitcases on top of his head with as much ease as though he was putting on a hat, and then proceeded to climb several flights of stairs. I followed with amazement, thinking that an effort like that on my part would at least end up in a whip lash and several treatments by a chiropractor.

By this time, I was quite stiff and rather pooped after having gotten no sleep for almost forty eight hours, so I popped a pill to make sure I got a full eight hours and passed out rather quickly on the single bed that had been provided for me. It was nice to have a bed again.

January 20th

This morning I was up and had a nice cold shower (as there was no hot water), and was down in the lobby, bag and baggage waiting to be picked up at 8:00 A.M. as promised. I decided to journal while I waited and was thinking about how I had just dragged, pulled and pushed over 175 pounds of luggage over 12,000 km. (well actually, I didn't drag it over the ocean – but you get the picture). I was not even charged an extra fee for the excess weight. Most of the contents were going to be left in Ghana anyway.

As I sat waiting, I couldn't help but feel the growing heat in the lobby. The tiny air-conditioner was working at full capacity, but with the doors swinging to and fro continuously, it just couldn't keep up. I was full of anticipation and trying to keep still so that I wouldn't perspire too much with the rising heat. I wanted to at least (for the translator who was picking me up) look like I was well rested and relaxed. I don't do well in the heat. I watched the people passing by the front gate - women carrying heavy loads on top of their heads, and little boys on their way to peddle some wares. People seemed so relaxed and happy. It reminded me somewhat of Mexico and yet there was something different about these people.

Two hours later I was greeted by a friendly lady by the name of Patience, who was an advocate for the rights of women and children and employed by I.N. Network in Ghana. I was told in advance that Patience would be meeting me, and that she was a wonderful lady. She apologised for being late, and said that she had a touch of malaria and was not feeling well. It was kind of like someone saying that they had a touch of the flu (in N. America). Still, she took me for lunch at a lovely outdoor Ghanaian smorgasbord in Accra, with probably a dozen or more local dishes. I tried to sample a bit of everything. It all was very tasty, but I didn't have the stomach to try the goat soup, even though it did look just fine and everyone else seemed to be enjoying it.

As we drove through the streets of Accra to the I.N. office, I was saddened at the poverty that I saw everywhere. I had been to Mexico several times, but had never seen anything like this. Everywhere in the streets there were young children and youth who should have been in school. They were selling everything you could possibly need or want, from gum and tropical fruit to African artwork and beautiful batik cottons. As far as the eye could see, there were vendors. Some of them had little stands set up on the roadside and others carried their small stands on their heads, where they sold their wares from. They would surround the cars, and the drivers would roll their windows down to wheel and deal. A deal would be struck amidst the masses of vehicles and pedestrians moving in the streets. The vendors would run along side the vehicles, or in front of them in order to finish the sale. Traffic kept moving. If one vendor had the attention of a driver for a potential sale, hordes of other vendors would swarm around the rest of the passengers in the vehicle. The vendors were very courteous (and persistent) and never got angry over a lost *sale, and no one got upset with the vendors all over the road, but I certainly was thankful that I was not driving. This is what they were used to. This was life in Accra.*

I especially noticed the handicapped people trying to sell items on the streets. If they were not capable of selling, they begged. There were no soup kitchens in Accra and no homeless shelters either. Everyone was on their own, if they had no family or friends that were able to help. One fellow in particular caught my eye. The only way that I can think of describing him, is that he was running along like a three legged dog, with one deformed leg hanging useless by his side. The other leg was bent so out of shape that he wasn't able to stand upright. He was running along beside another vendor, and what really amazed me was that he was chatting and laughing with the fellow who was walking along side him. There was no "pity party." He seemed to be getting on with his life to the best of his abilities. He could certainly teach the rest of us a thing or two about life. He was also working as a vendor.

The streets and alleys were strewn with garbage, as I understood that there was no garbage pick up like we have in North America. Where were they supposed to put the garbage? It was just dropped on the ground and fell where it would, and then was trampled underfoot by others who seemed to be oblivious to the fact that it was even there.

I saw some children searching through huge containers of garbage for anything that was salvageable and could be sold or eaten, while other children walked to school in tidy clean uniforms. Education is not free in Ghana, so the majority of children do not get an education unless they are from a wealthy home, or are sponsored by people in other countries. I saw four or five small children playing on an old abandoned "pink" car that had been stripped clean. It was only a shell and the children were crawling in and out the empty windows and seemingly having a great time.

I wondered if there were any "American" fast food restaurants in that city of over four million people. We hear that McDonald's is world wide now, so I figured they must have an outlet in a city of that size, but I saw nothing that even vaguely resembled a hamburger "joint." I actually don't think that they would be able to stay in business with the poverty that I witnessed in Accra.

Ghanaians view their country as a Christian country. The latest poll showed that 85 % of the people in Accra go to church. The poll covered anyone who believed in Christ, which included the Catholics, Protestants, Baptists, Evangelicals, Pentecostals, Charismatics, Mormons and Jehovah Witnesses, etc. It seemed as though everyone had faith. Cars were decorated with sayings like, "Jesus Lives" or "Trust God" etc. I saw lots of little brightly coloured food stands with names such as, "King Jesus – Rice and Beans" or "My Redeemer Lives – Yams and Chicken." These were the fast food restaurants on the sides of the roads. The enthusiasm with their faith really impressed me. They were certainly not ashamed of what they had. On the contrary, they talked about their faith openly. It was a big part of their lives. Even the secular radio station talked about praising God, between playing the old sixties Beatle's tunes and the local Ghanaian hits. Talking about God was an everyday part of their lives. They depended on him for everything.

There were churches everywhere in all parts of Ghana, however, in the villages where there were shrines and fetish priests, the traditional religion was practiced which is believed to have originated with the practice of voodoo.

Their traditional religion has many gods. There are gods of vengeance, gods of fertility, gods of healing, and so on. Some shrines may have 77 gods while other villages and shrines may have 65 or any other amount. The number varies from shrine to shrine. There is not just one Holy God who is all powerful and loving and can do nothing but good, as we believe as evangelical Christians. Some of their gods are quite nasty to say the least, and their demonic power is very real to them.

We finally arrived at the I.N. Network Office and I was introduced to the various friendly staff members and then waited for the arrangements to be made, and odd jobs to be done before we left again. I wondered how many visitors passed through those doors in the last year. I was introduced to the Rev. Walter Pimpong, who seemed incredibly tired, or maybe even ill. I remember thinking that he must be awfully bored with me, as I was putting the poor man to sleep. His eyes kept closing during our short conversation. After he prayed with me, he told me what a long hard week they had the week before, as there had been a lot of visitors. It was then that I understood why he appeared to be nodding off in my presence. The poor fellow was overworked, and then came back for more. I heard that at one time Walter Pimpong had been offered a job with the Billy Graham Ministries in the USA; however Rev. Pimpong felt that God was calling him back to Ghana to work with the trokosis.

I waited quite some time for the staff to decide what to do with me, and to arrange for a vehicle to take me to the Adidome Training Centre in the Volta Region. I was paying close attention to the posters and signs that were plastered all over the inside of the offices. They were all about the rights of women and children in Ghana. Some said that children should be in school, not forced into

37

labour. Others spoke against female circumcision, and then some posters told of the jail sentence that one would receive for buying sex with young girls. I could see that they were a mighty force for the rights of Ghanaian women and children.

Once we stepped outside again, I noticed a young girl in the back seat of a truck. She had been picked up by one of the staff (of another organization who shared the same building as I.N.) who was concerned about the girl's well-being, as she was selling herself on the street for some much needed money. She was tiny and frail looking and didn't look any older than ten or eleven but she was actually fourteen years old. The worker who picked her up was quickly introduced to me, and then she told me to go and talk to the girl, as we had the same first name. I felt a little awkward as I didn't know how much English the little girl knew, but I proceeded to do as I was instructed. When I approached the vehicle I squatted down to "Linda's" level and told her that was my name too. I tried a little bit of chit-chat and then asked her if she knew what our name meant, and then said that it was a Spanish name that meant beautiful and that she was indeed beautiful, etc. Her father had been found and was sitting beside her and kept trying to reinforce the fact that she was beautiful. All the while I talked, Linda cried. The father was very concerned about his daughter, but couldn't supply the things that she needed, and so she tried selling herself. She wasn't a seasoned prostitute by any means and had a soft heart. I felt that she was ashamed to be picked up for prostituting. I didn't think that my chat with her had much impact, as I didn't understand the customs and practices of the people in that country, but as a foster parent and a mother my heart went out to her.

Once again, we were off and back to the same hotel for another night. I was told we would leave for the Adidome Training Centre in the Volta Region the following day as I don't believe that a vehicle was available yet. I did ask what the plans were for Linda, and was told that a social worker would council her about STD's and AIDS, etc. and she would be sent on her way – with not so much as a piece of bread, or a bowl of soup. There were no youth shelters, foster homes or any other kind of help for any children in Ghana. There were no soup kitchens or any other free food for those who were hungry. Young people came to the city in droves to try and make a better life for themselves, only to find a life full of hunger, danger and a fear of what they didn't know.

January 21ˢᵗ

I was anxious to get to the Adidome Training Centre to start doing interviews with some of the liberated trokosis, as that is what I came to Ghana for, but due to the fact that there was no available vehicle, it looked like I would be spending another day in Accra. I was given another apology and told that there would be a vehicle available the following day. Patience phoned the hotel to ask how I was doing and told me to let her know if I needed anything. I understood that things were sometime unavoidable, so that was fine. I certainly didn't mind spending another day in Accra.

Since I was staying in Accra for an extra day, I decided to hire a taxi to take me to the beach area, as well as to the African Art Museum (a place where vendors sell their African arts, crafts and fabrics). One of the front desk clerks told me that she knew someone who was very honest (it was probably a friend or relative) and would stay with me for 10 Cedi an hour. Our Canadian money was about the equivalent of the Ghanaian money so it was easy enough to figure out. I thought that was a reasonable price, so arrangements were made and we were off. The taxi driver spoke a bit of English and I could understand if I listened real hard. I think he had to listen to me as well, as I was the one with the accent in Accra and I speak rather quickly. He told me what his name was and it was so long and complicated, all I got out of it was Emanuel, so that was his name for the afternoon. I was called, "Mama" which is a term of endearment or respect. I tried asking him about the trokosis, but he either didn't understand me, or didn't really know anything about them, after all the custom of trokosis were shrouded in secrecy. Many Ghanaians don't know that they even exist.

We started out for the ocean and while winding and weaving perilously through the treacherous traffic and vendors we engaged in some conversation - that was when we weren't talking to the vendors. I asked him questions about anything and everything that I saw along the way and he was only too happy to tell me all about "his" wonderful Ghana, and how blessed they were to have a president who was an evangelical Christian. Atta Evans Mills had been elected just 2 days before I left for Ghana and the people were so happy about that. I had noticed in the local newspaper, an article that read: "Oh, What an Obama Day Today Is!" They were elated that Obama had been elected in the USA. Emanuel said how good it was for them to live in a peaceful country that was not war torn.

We finally made it to the beach. I took my camera with me and Emanuel insisted on carrying the empty camera case. I think he felt special with that case as it looked like it could have a camera in it. I must say that it did look good on him.

The ocean was very impressive (as most oceans are) and as far as the eye could see, there was water and sand (and garbage). I stood in the warmth of the rolling waves as they crashed about my feet and threatened to drag me back in to the sea. I spotted an odd looking fishing boat way out in the water and took a photo with the zoom lens. It was a beautiful day – hot, overcast, but beautiful. I bought Emanuel and I bottled pineapple drinks and we sat on the beach furniture in the shade of an old umbrella to just watch and listen to the waves. It was really awesome, but on the other hand I could see all the broken beach furniture that had no graveyard to go to, as well as a lot of garbage waiting to be drawn back into the ocean. I could tell that Emanuel was having a nice afternoon too. I am sure that he would rather be at the beach than driving through the traffic and vendors. He certainly didn't mind "babysitting" me.

At one point, four Ghanaian police officers strolled by fairly close to where we were relaxing. They were holding what looked like machine guns. The vendors in the area told me that they were Russian machine guns and laughed at my naivety. I was going to go closer to get a picture of them, but one vendor warned me that it was illegal to take photos of police officers or government officials, so I took a picture when they weren't looking. The vendors looked nervous, but I assured them that I wasn't seen.

In the meantime a young lady by the name of Victoria came up to me and offered to give me a foot massage and paint my toe nails for 10 Cedi (a lot). I agreed as I was just sitting there and had a bit of money to waste. She didn't look like she was suffering from poverty by the look of her clothing and style, but it was nice to get pampered. I joked about what a "white" foot I had, and they laughed heartily. While I was having that done, other vendors saw the chance to try and sell me things, since I couldn't get up and go anywhere with wet nails. I ended up buying a few beaded necklaces and a purse made out of a coconut that was rather unusual. The vendors were genuinely friendly. They wanted to know about where I was from and what it was like in Canada. We sat on the beach chairs and chatted for an hour or so. I showed them my little family photo album. They were intrigued with the pictures of snow. Their English was pretty good and they could understand me too.

After that, we were on our way to the African Art Museum to shop. I do wish that I had stayed longer and bartered more at the market, but it was a zoo! It was even hard to get inside as all the vendors outdoors were trying to nab me in the process to show me their wares. There were not many visitors there and since I was the token white person, I guess I was up for grabs. The booths were only 3 or 4 feet wide and it seemed as though there were more vendors than booths. I didn't have a clue what I was looking for and I wasn't left alone to check things out, compare prices or stop and think about what I wanted to purchase. They were on me like flies on honey, or stink on a skunk (I could have smelled like one as the heat was awful). I felt claustrophobic. I couldn't think – they wouldn't let me! I only went down one row and bought a few items under duress (mostly from the same vendor at the end of the row) and then decided to get out of there – fast! On the way out, I spotted an African shirt that I thought my oldest son would like and quickly made the purchase. After getting out in the open, a fellow in a wheel chair trapped me, so I bought 3 bracelets that he had made out of old Ghanaian money.

I thought I would be safe or at least left alone in the taxi, but the vendors were tapping on the windows with their hand carved elephants, and beating their drums saying, "Free. Free." When they got my attention, they would say, "Only 5 Cedi Madame." Again, none of the vendors were rude in any way, but I did see discouragement in their faces when I didn't keep buying their wares. Selling their wares was how they made their living.

I was very glad to get back to the little hotel after a few hours where I soon received a phone call from Patience, reminding me that she was there to help in any way. I told her about my afternoon and that I had a good time, and that she should do what she had to do and not worry about me. She let me know that we would definitely be leaving for the training centre in the morning and that I would be picked up at 10:00 A.M. It sounded good to me.

I had some much needed quiet time in my hotel room and did some journaling and then decide to try some Ghanaian food in the hotel restaurant. Since the place was empty- except for me- I was waited on by both waitresses. I ordered a Ghanaian dish - something that had chicken, green peppers, carrots and onions that were in a gravy-like sauce. I was the only one in the restaurant and so I read a bit while waiting for my dinner. Within twenty minutes my Ghanaian dish arrived. Mmmmmmm! It was very presentable and looked very good. I very carefully took a piece of chicken and some veggies, dipped it into the harmless looking sauce, opened my mouth, wrapped my lips around it and proceeded to chew. Instantly, I knew that those green peppers were something that I was not familiar with, as my mouth was on fire! I had the capability of setting the place on fire as I was sure that flames were exploding out of every crevice on the lower part of my face! My eyes bugged out, as both waitresses asked me if I was okay and all I could do for the moment was wave at them while blowing flames from my open mouth (or at least what felt like flames) and try to smile. A couple of Ghanaian fellows came by my table and started chuckling, and then the chef came out to apologize for the hot spices. They thought that I knew what I was ordering. I thought I knew too. I didn't want to singe the ear hairs off the chef, so I took a quick drink of Sprite and exclaimed, "Boy that was hot!" I decided that it was going to take me a few hours to get this meal down, so took it to my room and worked at it for the balance of the evening. It did take a few hours, but I ate every bit of it. It was really very tasty, but much too hot for this Canadian; however, it was the tastiest meal that I had in the two weeks that followed.

January 22nd

Well, today was the day that we were finally going to the Adidome Training Centre and I was really looking forward to it. After a good two hours of travelling time of going through various towns and villages, we finally arrived at the compound. The countryside was very dry and there were road blocks set up here and there with police officers or soldiers on guard. No one bothered us. We drove across to the other side of the Volta River to get to our destination.

Everyone was happy to see Patience (Auntie Pat) and I was politely introduced to the staff individually. I was taken for a quick tour of some of the classes, where some of the students would stand and welcome me with a short song. Others just welcomed me in English. There were about one hundred and fifty students of the female gender only, with around twenty children under the age of two. Some of the students were married and their children would stay in the nursery while classes were on. Their spouses were left behind in their villages. Several of the cooking students were middle aged widows who had no way of taking care of themselves and would have starved if it wasn't for the fact that they were learning a trade so they could support themselves in the future. The young mothers would carry their babies in slings on their backs after classes were over and when I tried to approach some of the little ones, they would cry or stare at me in horror! They were afraid of me. They had never seen a white lady before. After a while (a week or more), I was able to chat to some of them and even pick them up. All of the babies were simply adorable!

The students were learning hairdressing, dressmaking, bread making, beading, weaving, soap making, mat making, etc. and they all worked so hard to learn what they could. They were so happy to be getting an education. A lot of the girls could not read or write, but they could learn a trade. I noticed that everyone walked at a slower pace. No one was in a real hurry and I think it was because of the intense heat (and no one wore a watch). I sure didn't feel like moving any faster than at a snails pace in that awful heat either – just not my thing, thank you very much.

After having a tour of the school, someone decided that I just might be hungry and went to prepare dinner while I checked out my little guest room, which was really more than adequate – at least when the power was on, the air-conditioner worked. For the time being, the power was off, so I used the time to set up my mosquito net before it got dark outside and got my emergency flashlight out of my back pack, just in case. I couldn't figure out where the rods went into the top of the net, but it covered my bed and I figured that it would suffice, just the way it was. Since the power was out and I was bored, I sat under my mosquito net with the flashlight and reminisced about the forts I made for my boys when they were little. I was called to dinner by Patience rapping on my door. We ate rice interspersed with the odd bean, and a tomato sauce that had a few veggies in it. It was quite enjoyable, but I was too hot to eat much. After we ate and chatted a bit about getting some trokosi interviews set up, I noticed that it had gotten dark within just a fifteen minute time gap and by 6:30 P.M. it was completely dark outside. There was no time for a Canadian sunset. It was light or dark – no in between. The power was still off, so I couldn't use the air conditioning. That night I fell asleep in my guest room with a battery operated fan that I brought along. It was none too powerful and in order to get some relief from the heat, I set it about four inches from my face. It worked, as I dozed off quite quickly. It used four D batteries and since I only brought one extra set of that size battery, I hoped that the power would come on in the next few days.

The next morning I was quite excited about doing interviews that day only to discover that a lot of the liberated trokosis or their children who were born at the shrines were either too shy to talk to me, or else they felt it was emotionally too painful and they found it too hard to share and dig up the past. Some of them didn't know what my motives were as a stranger. Sometimes they would suffer some depression for some time after giving their testimony. I did sympathize with their situations, but getting their stories was why I had come to Ghana, and I could see that it would take some doing on God's part, as I didn't know where to begin. I thought that I was going to get a story just the way it was told, without asking questions. That was not going to happen. Patience was doing her best trying to arrange for some of the liberated trokosis that she knew – and she knew a lot - to give me some interviews. She really was trying hard to get me some interviews. I was beginning to see that it wasn't going to be an easy task. God was going to have to intervene on our behalf.

Nothing happened that day. I just wandered all over the compound and smiled and waved at the little children. I met Rose, the school nurse who had been a nurse for the government for most of her life. Now she was retired and getting "peanuts" for a pension so she worked for I.N. on the compound, and as a school nurse in other areas. Her English was good and she was a lovely lady. She was very friendly and would approach me if she saw me walking alone and strike up a quick conversation. I felt that she was a warm, caring person and obviously a great nurse. The students would smile or wave back, but they were so shy. I actually felt a little lonely and even a little awkward hanging around and not knowing what to do with my time or who to talk to. Not too many of the students spoke English, as it was their second language.

Patience asked me later in the evening if I would be interested in doing an interview with a fetish priest or two. She suggested that we go out to the village of Kebanu and meet the two fetish priests there, who had given up their trokosis about twelve years ago. I was a little apprehensive, even though I did want to have the experience of meeting them. I guess she could see by my facial expression that I wasn't sure how to conduct that interview. I had just never thought that I would be asked if I wanted to interview a fetish priest and it caught me off guard. I think Patience thought that I might judge them since they were still practicing voodoo, etc. even though they liberated their trokosis. It was decided that we would go to Kebanu the following day.

I decided to do a bit of reading and journaling in my room and then get another good night sleep. I could hear the sound of drums coming from the other side of the Volta River, and it was strangely eerie to me. They got louder during the evening and then even louder music was heard as well – African voices. I was curious about the drums and the villages over there. On this side of the river, all the trokosis had been liberated - not so on the other side. I found out that the fetish priests and elders on the other side of the Volta River were quite hostile and had put guards around the villages to keep anyone from forcefully taking, or even talking to their trokosis, but now I am getting ahead of myself.

International Needs has an office in this building in Accra. The rest of the building is shared by other Christian aid organizations.

These posters were plastered on the office walls of International Needs, stressing the rights of women and children. .

An old torn poster advocating the rights of women and girls

Masses of shoppers and vendors in the streets of Accra - I was sure glad that I wasn't doing the driving, as everyone seemed oblivious to the cars or the vendors on the roads.

A vendor selling African carvings in the streets of Accra - Patience bought the carving on the left to use in counselling girls not to keep quiet when they are sexually abused.

An abandoned fast food stand in Accra - There were no fast food restaurants, as we know them.

A young girl selling small bags of drinking water beside the road

A vendor's booth at the African Art Museum in Accra

*A vendor carving masks in his booth - He wasn't happy
that I took his picture without asking first.*

The four heavily armed police officers on the beach

This is a large strange looking fishing vessel out on the ocean. I don't believe it was motorized. The overcast skies were because of the North West winds blowing very fine sand into Ghana.

Chapter 3

The Fetish Priest

It was the morning to go and visit the village of Kebanu. Patience had arranged for me to interview a fetish priest in the village, as he seemed okay with the idea. Patience had to pay him 30 cedi (about $30.00 Canadian) in order for me to ask him some questions and get some answers in return. We also had to drive to several places in some of the little towns to try and find someone who sold Schnapps, as we were told that the fetish priest would not see us if we didn't bring some bottles of hard liquor. He needed it to invoke the gods, before he could agree to the interview, and had to use Schnapps, apparently. I have no idea if it was their god's drink of choice or the fetish priest's preference.

I should go back to the night before. I had no idea that Patience was trying to get the fetish priests to agree to go through an interview with me. That evening she asked if I would be interested, and I said that I would. I must admit that I was a little apprehensive, as I didn't know what to expect with regards to custom, culture, voodoo ceremonies, etc. and Patience saw that I was apprehensive. She asked if I was afraid and I told her that I wasn't, but that I wanted to do things in a way that I wouldn't offend their culture or rituals, etc. She asked me to give her a list of questions and she would check them to see if they were appropriate. I did so, and she said they were fine. That night I read in a devotional book about how God does not allow us to choose who we can be compassionate to, but expects us to get up out of our comfort zone and minister to those people we would ordinarily shun. That spoke to my heart, and I felt that God had a reason for me to go to Kebanu the next day. I felt much calmer about going and was actually rather excited to be visiting with the locals in a village, and was especially excited about speaking with a fetish priest.

I was told by Patience that the fetish priest would not sit for long to do an interview, so I decided that I had better be prepared to do the interview quickly and ask the proper questions. I prayed that God would help me speak to him with some wisdom, as I didn't have a clue about how I was going to conduct this interview in my own strength.

It seemed that wherever we traveled, some others needed a ride part way or even farther. Today, a Bible School student sat beside me in the back seat of the vehicle as though we were canned sardines. I always had to take so much "stuff" like camera, audio recorder, water, food and even bathroom tissue and some candy and a few toys for the children. That overloaded backpack usually had to sit on my lap, for lack of space. They were a generous bunch though, always offering to help with driving others or dropping off supplies. The Bible School student was a very interesting young man and we talked about anything and everything, and rather enjoyed each others company. I think that we each found the other one rather interesting. He was a very sincere young man with regards to what he felt God had in store for him. I can't remember his name, unfortunately. It was hard to remember everyone's name as they were so long and difficult to pronounce. Most of the locals had an English name in there somewhere that was easier to remember. I learned that one could tell where a person was from; who there father was, if they were a twin, etc. etc. just from their name. When you were given a name at birth, it gave a lot of history. Yet, no one kept track of actual birth dates. Chatting with him made the two hour road trip seem a lot shorter.

We left for Kebanu around 10:30 in the morning ,as we didn't want to arrive while the women were still in the fields. They would get up at the crack of dawn or even earlier and work in their fields until noon when the hot African sun was too unbearable, and then they would head back to the village to rest awhile and start other chores.

I was told that the villagers had no food to offer us – not even a cup of tea - so we would have to bring our own snacks and water if we wanted to eat during the day. I brought a few goodies, but most of the time I found that it was just too hot to eat. Water seemed to suffice.

We met with the elders of the village first, and they very hospitably put some plastic lawn chairs in a large circle, so that we could get through the formal greetings, visit a bit, and then take care of business. One of the older elders came out with a beach towel resting on top of his head and hanging over his shoulders. I assumed that he needed that to keep the sun off his head – made sense to me. Patience introduced me while the chairs were being set out and everyone there shook my hand and said, "Welcome." I did feel welcomed – a bit awkward as I didn't speak the language– but welcomed, none the less. Most of the elders knew some English and were happy to try it out on me. They were a friendly bunch. I guess that I was a bit of a novelty as well.

The children kept coming over to check me out, as they were curious as to why a white lady would be in their village. They were all so cute. I gave some of them some little metal cars, and that made the children multiply. They came out from behind every hut that was there, smiling and pointing to another child, who didn't yet have a car. The adult women kept shooing them away, but they weren't too interested in leaving, as they might miss out on something. Some of the children were stark naked, as they had no clothing to put on. Others were half dressed in torn t-shirts with no pants and then other children were fully clothed. None of them wore sandals or flip-flops that I noticed. One little toddler had a mess of scabs on his chin that looked very sore. It covered his chin completely and was infected right up to his lower lip and out towards his cheeks. I asked the mother if he fell and she just answered that it was a disease, and that he kept picking at it, as it was very itchy. It looked like impetigo to me. She lovingly cradled him on her lap. She couldn't afford to get medical treatment for him, but fortunately International Needs had arranged for medical staff from Canada to come out every so often, to visit the villages and treat the afflicted.

Before anything was allowed to be discussed, a quick formal greeting had to be exchanged, out of courtesy and tradition. The visiting person would ask three questions with regards to how the parents, family and the person (being addressed) were doing, and the person questioned would answer (with one affirmative word) to all three questions. On the last question they would say something incidental like, "My mother wasn't feeling well this week." The visitor would answer with something appropriate. Then the tables were turned, and the villager would ask the same questions of the visitor and would also get similar answers. After that introduction, the visitor would state why she/he was there, and the informal visiting would commence. Being a Canadian, I noticed that the Ghanaians also said,"eh" and awful lot, but when Canadians say, "eh?"- it is more like a question. The Ghanaians said, "Ayyyy....." in a long drawn out way. I was curious to know if it meant the same thing, and was told that it was a way of affirming something that the other person was saying, such as, "Really" or "I hear you."

I must say that unfortunately most of our manners disappeared in North America during the 1970's with the hippie generation, so I was so impressed at the manners and politeness of the Ewe tribe and the Ghanaian people in general. They were very likeable.

After all the greetings were over and done with, Patience was able to ask about how the villagers were doing, and then, why we were there. We asked (or rather Patience asked) their permission to interview the fetish priest and we were granted an audience with him. Actually, it had been arranged in advance, but we still had to go through all the formalities. We all got up and moved to the other side of the village where the chairs were once again put out. This time we met across from the large tree that the fetish priest was sitting under. The heat was just bearable, while we sat under the shade of the tree. The priest was a fine looking specimen sitting on a beautifully hand carved stool, with his priestly robes, etc. He wore shell beads around both wrists and ankles. His feet wrapped in sandals rested on what looked like a goat skin rug. He had nice big teeth, although somewhat yellowed in colour, they seemed well taken care of. He was a nice looking man with a wonderful smile and a hearty laugh. His calico (all white) robe was thrown over his left shoulder and hung down to the ground. The other shoulder was bare. He wore a hat (that looked like an upside down basket) and had a braided rope around his neck which fell to the ground from where he sat. He also held a dagger of some sort in his hand, which was part of his priestly garb. He didn't look any older than 25 years, but apparently was considerably older. I liked him at once, but tried to hide the fact that I was still a little nervous about doing the interview, just because I hadn't been in a situation like this before. It wasn't familiar to me.

The quick formal greeting was also repeated in this circle, and then the fetish priest had to invoke the spirits to see if it would be okay to speak with me. This is where the Schnapps came in.

I was not allowed to take photos at this time as we hadn't asked permission yet, so I couldn't photograph the ritual that was performed, however, it was etched into my mind quite clearly.

One of the fellows from the village rolled up his pants, took off his western t-shirt and removed a clean piece of colourful African printed fabric from the clothes line behind us, then wrapped it around his waist so it resembled a long skirt of some sort. He took the bottle of Schnapps and ritualistically poured three separate amounts into a small wooden bowl that the fetish priest held out. The priest started the ritual by saying (what I assumed was) a one or two minute prayer in Ewe and then proceeded to ceremoniously pour the Schnapps onto the ground in front of him, again, in three separate "pours" all the while saying something to the gods. I understood that he was "calling up the deities" or the gods, to see if it was okay to give me an interview. Apparently, it went well, as I did get the interview from him. The fellow in the long "skirt" just waited in a squatting position for more gestures from the priest. I think that he felt it was a privilege to serve the fetish priest in this way, although I am not sure what his position was. Maybe he was a fetish priest in training.

Once again, the small wooden bowl was held up and it was filled with Schnapps, but this time, it was done in one gesture. The priest appeared to me to be taking a drink, but was only holding it in his mouth. All of a sudden, and with great skill, he blew the Schnapps out of his mouth in a fine mist that I am sure was at least three feet wide, three feet deep and three feet high! Fortunately, I was sitting about eight feet away, so I wasn't physically affected and stayed dry. I wanted to say," Wow!" but held my tongue. This blowing -of - the - Schnapps was repeated two more times, and after each time he communicated something else to his gods. When he was finished, he took the braided rope that was tied around his neck, and swished it several times over the Schnapps that he had poured onto the ground in front of him. He did all this while being seated and I noticed that no one was paying too much attention to the ceremony. Most of the elders were looking around at what everyone else was doing. I was rather expecting a twirling voodoo dance in masks and grass skirts similar to what I had seen in movies when I was much younger, but that didn't happen, much to my relief. They passed the Schnapps around and held out a glass to me with about an ounce or two of the hard liquor in it. I did read the label on the box while on the drive out to Kebanu and made a mental note that it had an alcohol content of 55 %. I remember thinking that it would certainly disinfect any wound. As a non drinker-not even a social drinker- I had no idea that they were going to offer a glass of the brew to me. Since I wasn't sure what the appropriate thing to do was (as I didn't want to offend them and get chased out of the village) I took the drink and swallowed some of it. It was nasty to say the least and it burned my throat. Without realizing it, I made a terrible face and that struck them funny, so they all had a good laugh at my expense. It was an ice-breaker as I passed the glass back with a silly smile on my face.

That was the end of the ritual and then it was okay to state (officially) why I was there, and what I wanted from them. Patience didn't really want me to share with them that I was writing a book, as they might feel exploited. Now it was my turn to speak, and I found it was a bit awkward because I wanted to say things that would be acceptable in their culture. Patience was translating for me, so I am sure that she got the point across in the way it was intended. Patience had told me in advance that if I offended them, they would drive us out of the village, and I didn't want that to happen. That was the reason she asked to look at my question and answer interview sheet.

I told the young fetish priest – who's name was Togbe Mama Venornuah that I was in Ghana to get some information on the culture of the trokosis, that most of my information I had gotten from other sources, and that I thought it would be good to get some first hand information directly from a fetish priest – or in other words, the other side of the story. I also said that I would write only what he told me. He was quite cheerful and laid back and joked in Ewe to the others sitting in the circle, then agreed to the interview. I asked him if he wanted to just give me a story, or if he would rather have me ask him some questions. He chose to have me ask him questions. I understood that he would not sit too long for me, so I really didn't ask him all that I wanted, but I did get some information from him. He was willing to talk and seemed quite honest with his answers. After I returned to the guest house, I thought of a lot more things that I would have liked to have discussed with him, but it was too late. When I left for Ghana, I had no idea that I would be interviewing a fetish priest while there. Had I known, I would have been better prepared and would have given it a lot more consideration. The following are my questions and the priest's answers. The interview is as accurate as I could get it, directly from the fetish priest.

Q. How did you become a fetish priest? Is it something that is passed down from one generation to another, or is it something that you choose?

A. It is a calling. An incident happened to me when I was young. I had disappeared for days and no one could find me. Later I was found face down in the reeds of the Volta River. I had drowned and was underwater. The gods protected me and I was revived. They (the villagers who found him) then went to the seers and it was predicted that I would become a fetish priest. A revelation came from the deities through the seers, and I was groomed and taught by the elders of the shrine and by the gods themselves. We have no record of births in the Ewe culture, but I would say that I have been a fetish priest for about 25 years.

Q. Wow! You don't look much older than 25 years. You must have been very young when you became a priest (to this he laughed heartily – they all did).

I read that the position of the fetish priest was more or less that of a police officer or a judge, to keep crime to a minimum in the villages. The priest was to keep social behaviours in tact. Is that true?

A. That is true.

Q. I understand that initially, animals were given to the fetish priest to atone for sin or crime. When did virgin girls start to take the place of animals?

A. This is a very old culture. We don't keep records so I don't know, but the gods demanded a virgin girl – not humans. We obeyed the gods or deities and did what they asked, or told us to do.

Q. Did the perpetrators or offenders have to pay for their crimes as well, or did the little virgin girls have to atone for everything? Was there a penalty that had to be paid by the perpetrators too?

A. Yes, but we cannot divulge some things to you, as some of our practices are secretive, and we must keep them that way.

I could see that I was only going to get answers about him, and not anything related to the shrine or the trokosis. The questions that I wanted to ask would have offended him if I kept pushing. There is a very real fear of the gods even for the fetish priests, as they know the powers that they are dealing with. I decided to keep everyone friendly and make this short. I also felt that I would get more information from the liberated trokosis than from the fetish priests.

Q. Do you think that International Needs has been fair in their dealings with you?

A. Initially, we did not think it was fair. As fetish priests we represent the deities, and so we had to come to an understanding and communicate with the deities to make them happy. The gods were satisfied with the final deal that we made, but again we cannot talk about the secrecy of our deities.

Q. How do you feel about the Christian God?

A. We believe in the same God, creator of heaven and earth, but where you go through Jesus to get to God, we pray directly to God to get to the deities. We have many gods, but you have only one.

Q. We all have regrets in life and say that if we could change something, or do something over again it would be this or that. If you could change anything regarding your past or your life, what would it be?

A. That was a wise question. The gods decide how we live so we obeyed the deities and did what they told us to do, so I couldn't change anything, but (he sat there and thought for a moment or two while we waited quietly) I would like to have better living conditions and a better home for my family and villagers (and he pointed to his mud hut with a thatched roof, and then waved his hand over the village).

I thanked him for his time, and thought that he really did not want a lot. They had no electricity, no running water, no basics. It looked like their living conditions hadn't changed for centuries. The buildings and homes at

Kebanu (like other similar villages) were made out of mud bricks with thatched roofs and cut out openings for windows to let the air in and out. The shrine was no different as far as construction went. It was made of mud with a thatched roof too, but had a little, white, painted, short, mud wall around it. One had to look hard to even locate it. The shrines are not much different from the villager's mud huts. The shrines are sacred and outsiders are not allowed in. If I had been allowed into a shrine I would have had to be cleansed by a ritual with their holy water and then I would have had to bow down to the idols out of respect. As a Christian I can't compromise. No picture taking is allowed inside a shrine either.

There were no welfare cheques and no handouts for anyone in Ghana. I wondered if they gave up their trokosis so that they could have a few more comforts, like good drinking water from a well, and schooling for their children. They would have had to be in dire straights to make a deal for clean water and schools. The Ghanaian people greatly value education, and sanitary water is a must to keep disease down to a minimum.

After we were finished our chat, I told him that I had a gift for him. Actually, I hadn't brought anything for a man, just feminine things that I could give in gift bags for the liberated trokosis that I was planning to interview, but then I thought of a new beach towel that I had brought along. It had a comical moose on it that was playing hockey, so I told him that I was from a city named Moose Jaw, and that hockey was our national sport. He laughed when I showed him, and put it over his one bare shoulder and then insisted that I take a picture of him, and asked me to send it to him in a frame.

Togbe Mama Venornuah's wife came by just then, and said, "We have to give the gods thanksgiving." Apparently, the story went that many children had just drowned that past week in a fishing boat accident on the Volta River. One mother called on the gods to save her children as they could not be found. Mysteriously they were found alive two days later, clinging to a tree at the edge of the river. So, she said, "The gods needed to be thanked." I guess that would be something they celebrated once we were gone.

In the following chapter you will read Arianna's story of her life as a trokosi in the village of Kebanu. It is brutal, and it was hard to realize that these same priests that I had interviewed in this village were the very same fetish priests who brought her so much pain and abuse. I do not doubt Arianna's story in the least, yet the fetish priests did not seem like monsters to me. I feel that perhaps under the demonic powers of the gods they serve, and with the "Schnapps" there was indeed horrific abuse (more than she was willing to share). As well, everyone knows that the fetish priests claim there are various gods, both good and evil, that serve various purposes. I was told that, by the fetish priest as I spoke with him. I feel their gods have blinded them from seeing what the one true God is capable of, with His unfathomless, unconditional love, and His great mercy and unlimited grace.

This was the dry season and the North West trade winds were blowing very fine sand from the Sahara desert into Ghana, so the skies always looked overcast as though it was about to rain, but it never did. We never felt any sand blowing into our faces or eyes. It was very subtle. The sun set within fifteen or twenty minutes at around 6:30 in the evening all year round and it rose at around 6:00AM right around the calendar. There were no late-light-outside evenings with a sunset. Because of the sand blowing in from the desert you could not even see any stars after dark. I am sure in a different season you would see the stars, but not during the dry season. It was intensely hot, but I never had to wear sun screen or sunglasses because of the overcast skies. The ground was so dusty and dry, and my feet were filthy after a few minutes of walking. The heat produced large drops of salty sweat that rolled off of my forehead and burned my eyes. My dry lips tasted of salt as well, and I realized how "spoiled" I was, longing for my comfortable old heritage home with the air conditioning and huge cast iron bathtub that I could relax in after a long day. I could curl up on my king sized bed with a nice cup of Chai tea with the T.V. or a good book just a few feet away. I do work hard every day, and don't often take much time to relax, but how much decadence do we live in, while other parts of the world live in deplorable conditions?

The Republic of Ghana is so poverty stricken. If not for donations from charity groups, wealthy people and churches from other countries, more people would starve to death, or die of disease. Ghanaians love their country, but the government is strapped by what I can see. They are proud of the fact that they are considered a Christian country with a Christian president. In talking with some of the locals, I was told that every politician that runs for office says that he will promote free education, but it never happens. Education is the key to prosperity, but it won't ever happen when the majority of Ghanaians are barely able to feed their families at best, much less send them to school. Unlike North America, all schools had uniforms. The uniforms in themselves just weren't affordable to most everyday Ghanaians.

We had to visit the old fetish priest of Kebanu before we left. That village had two shrines. The young priest represented the female deities, and the older priest represented the male deities – whatever that means. Togbe Tsadvmanuor was the name of the older fetish priest. He had been lying down as he wasn't feeling well. He looked rather weak, and was getting on in years. I felt sorry for him as he looked like he might not last too much longer, so I decided that I would not bother him with an interview (although, now I wish I had.) I think he was expecting me to get an interview from him as well, as he was also paid 30 cedi. He went through the same ritual as the young priest, and I noticed that they paid even less attention to him during the ceremony. I was able to take pictures in a subtle way while he did part of the ceremony. I figured that the first time I asked if I could take pictures should do for the rest of the visit.

When it came to the part where he was supposed to spray the Schnapps into the air, he didn't have enough energy and was too weak, so it just ran down his chin onto his white robe. When I first saw him, I immediately recognized him as the fetish priest in the photograph that Bev (the I.N. director in Canada) had sent me in an e-mail some time ago, but in the photograph he was much younger, more intimidating, fierce and powerful looking 12 years ago, than he was sitting in front of me today. He was fragile looking, old, and ill and really didn't look very scary at all.

We proceeded to visit and chat with the villagers and elders for quite some time. Everyone knew a little bit of English. Some of the elders could communicate quite well with me. One of them insisted on teaching me some Ewe words that I readily tried to repeat after him. I enjoyed their company and they all seemed like such a happy group despite their extreme poverty. They didn't give up on life as they knew it. I guess that things couldn't get much worse – in my opinion anyway – and they had hope for a brighter future. One lady was breast feeding her beautiful little baby, but he was more interested in staring at me than getting some nourishment. I was quite a novelty to the little ones.

Some of the elders who spoke fairly good English were very interested in my little family photo album that I had brought along. I showed them my photos with our big, old house covered in snow. The picture of my mom and dad went over very well. When I showed them their picture and said that my father was almost **88** years old and still in good health. They kept repeating, "How wonderful for you to have both your parents still living! God bless you!" Another photograph that went over well was of my friend Sharon (who is black) and her husband Rob (who is white) and their two mixed children. Also, I showed them a picture of our pastor who calls himself "the brown boy" because of his very dark skin colouring, and they were quite impressed. One elder, after finding out that I had eight children (who call me mom) thought that I was in excellent shape for having all those kids. I tried to explain that I had only given birth to two of them. Some were adopted and some were long term foster children. He didn't quite get that, as there are no foster homes in Ghana, but still he thought I looked pretty good for my age (I am sure that I didn't smell as good – but no one seemed to noticed) even with my hair, face and clothes wringing wet with sweat. I remembered then, my grade six teacher Mr. Dyck, who told me that boys sweat, and girls perspire. I would have liked to have had him see me in that village. I was definitely not perspiring. It was just plain sweat – nothing fancy.

All of the elders insisted on posing alone for a picture, and they all asked me to send them their photograph "in a frame." I was happy to do that, and I made sure that I mailed their orders the first week that I got home. They were a very nice group of villagers, and once I got comfortable and relaxed a bit, I had a very nice, interesting time. Overall, I felt quite honoured that they had accepted me so well. I liked them as well.

On the outskirts of Kebanu I was shown a well that had been put in, so that the villagers would have safe drinking water which made them a lot less susceptible to diseases. Within a short walk there was a school where the sponsored children could go. Both the well and the school had been part of the contract or agreement with the fetish priests and elders, when they agreed to liberate the trokosis from their shrines some ten or twelve years ago. The village was very grateful to International Needs, as they were in dire need of a well, school and sponsors. They also had women there who had attended the Adidome Training Centre who had been supplied with micro loans to run their own bakery (with an outdoor mud oven). I saw one lady selling her baked goods by the road, close to the school. All of the trokosis and their children, who had been liberated from the shrines in Kebanu had gotten counselling, rehabilitation, a trade, and then a micro loan from I.N. I heard it said that I.N. believed that the fetish priests should get counselling and rehabilitation as well, and I do think that may have been a good step towards understanding their fear with regards to the gods that they served.

We visited the school for a few minutes and I was so impressed by the clean uniforms and the good and courteous behaviour of the children. They crowded around me when they realized that I was taking pictures, and scrambled for a spot in the front. When I showed them their faces on the camera, they squealed with delight and laughed at themselves. The children who had sponsors in Canada put their hands up to show me who they were. They were the fortunate ones who were able to attend school because of the sponsors.

One little girl reached out and quickly rubbed my arm to see if it felt the same as her dark skin. That touched me.

When we got back in the vehicle, we were all pretty pooped I think – at least I was. No one said anything for a while. Pondering what I had just experienced in Kebanu, and being a rather impulsive person who quite often just blurts out her thoughts, I all of a sudden just said, "I liked that young fetish priest. He had a good sense of humour and he was very honest with the interview. He seemed like a nice enough fellow." I could hear instant relief in Patience's voice. I think she thought I was going to judge him, as some other foreigners may have done. She said that he was also a victim of his circumstances and environment, and I certainly agreed with her.

Earlier I had sensed some apprehension in Patience, with regards to my writing a book about the trokosis since I had never been to Africa before and knew nothing about their culture or language. Who was "I" to write about them? I saw such extreme poverty in Ghana. I knew that the people and organizations needed help from other countries, and they most certainly realized that as well, but were powerless to raise the funds themselves. They couldn't liberate trokosis without funds from sponsors in other wealthier countries. They were a proud people and would have liked to have been able to handle things without relying on others, yet they couldn't even afford to educate their own children. I do know that they did appreciate everyone who helped. I thought that a book about the trokosis might raise awareness and help in liberating more of them.

We were heading back to the Adidome compound for the night and had an extra passenger (again). We had picked up a woman by the name of Aku when we left the school. She was sitting next to me. Patience was engaging her in a conversation in Ewe and before I knew it, I was asked if I would like to interview her, as she was a liberated trokosi. Well, of course I wanted to! That was my first trokosi interview, so we stopped in the middle of the dirt road that we were travelling on. We got out of the vehicle and stood behind the truck. I clipped the microphone onto Patience so that we could begin. I guess that the reason we were doing the interview in the middle of the almost vacant road behind the truck, was because the driver was of the opposite sex and probably didn't want to hear what Aku was going to share. He just tipped back in his seat for a mid-day snooze.

As we started the interview and some picture taking, we noticed a woman down the road a few hundred feet who was yelling and making a big fuss with some men in the bushes. They were laughing at her, and she was obviously distraught about something. Aku was quite concerned about her, and was trying to ask Patience what the woman's problem was. Aku kept pointing at her and saying something in Ewe with concern in her voice. Now our interview was temporarily on hold. Patience, who could understand what the woman was hollering about, was saying that she thought the woman needed to go to the hospital. She seemed a little deranged to me, as she all of a sudden stripped right down to her birthday suit in the middle of the road, in full view of everyone, and then just dropped her clothing in a pile, on the dusty road. She saw me taking her picture and standing there stark naked, she smiled for the camera. Then, she partially dressed herself, put some fabric over one shoulder, and headed in our direction. Well, the interview wasn't going on at all by that time, so we just waited for the now half naked woman to join us. I didn't know what to expect. She started talking and complaining to Patience (as Patience spoke quite a few of the local languages) and I saw Patience give the woman one cedi (equivalent to one dollar). After that, the woman seemed a bit happier. Patience told me, that the woman had told her that she had no one to look after her, she was very hungry and had nothing to eat, and so she was depressed. With that information, I reached into my back pack and gave her everything I had brought along for the day, which were several pop-open cans of salmon, a few granola bars and some fruit snacks. Now she was truly happy! I realized that the cedi wouldn't buy her anything in that area, as we were in the middle of nowhere. There were no vendors on this road. She thanked me over and over, and still half naked with her underwear sticking out from the top of her shorts, she walked away with a huge smile on her face, and her hands full of cans of salmon. One would have thought that she had won the lottery! I figured that she was trying to sell herself to the men hidden in the bushes and they were making fun of her as she was an older woman.

We had lost a bit of time from the interview, and Aku was catching another ride into Accra to visit her children who were working there (as vendors, I think). Now we had to hurry with the interview as Aku's ride was not going to wait for us to finish, so we got down to business. I noticed that Aku had quite a large tattoo of numbers and letters on her left inside forearm. It was about six inches long and maybe three inches wide – very noticeable. I took a picture of the tattoo and asked when it was done. She said it was when she first was given as a trokosi, but she was so young that she didn't know anything about it. It was very similar to the tattoos given to the Jews (as identification) that were sent to the camps in the Second World War, but much larger. This is Aku's short story. Try as I might, I couldn't get a lot of details. She was a very nice lady, but just couldn't seem to give me what I wanted or needed. I think she had been so damaged that it was too hard for her to get into her old life, so she just told me in a way that wouldn't open up old wounds. Here is Aku's story.

I was the fifth child of seven in my family. I have no memories of being taken to the shrine, as I was so young. I must have been three or four years old – I'm not sure. When I first came to the shrine I was very small, so I didn't even know why I was there. As I got a little older, I would ask questions from the other trokosis as to why I lived there. No one could give me any information. I was told after I had been liberated, that a male relative of mine had an affair with a trokosi, which wasn't allowed, so I had been chosen by the gods to serve as a slave in the shrine, to atone for the crime of that relative. Apparently, my family had been cursed. I don't remember the ceremonies.

Life was so hard there as a trokosi that many times I thought about running away, but I was told by the fetish priest that I would die if I ran away and I believed it, even though I wasn't really living – just barely existing. There were about twenty or so trokosis living in that shrine and I would ask them questions about where I came from. They would tell me what they knew, but that wasn't much.

I was so unhappy there. I had no peace. I was so hungry all of the time. The starvation was awful. The fetish priest would go to the villagers to be fed if the produce in the fields wasn't enough and he would have a full stomach, but he never, ever provided for the trokosis in his shrine. If they had a good crop, he would sometimes give us a little, but it was usually sold to others. It didn't matter if we were fed or not as we could and would be replaced if we died. We weren't even as valued as a dog. Sometimes I would ask him for food as I was so weak from hunger, but he would just tell me in a casual voice that there wasn't any. I laboured in the fields of the shrine from dawn 'til dusk, even though sometimes I was too weak from malnutrition or disease. All of the trokosis were in the same position. I can't remember much physical abuse, as I blocked it all out. It is too painful to remember.

After I had my menstrual cycle, the fetish priest told me that he was going to have sex with me, as now I was considered a wife of the gods. There was nothing I could do about it. Suffering was all I had known. I had three children by him. One time when I was in child labour I was in the shrine, but I wasn't allowed to have the baby in there (even though that is where the trokosis lived and slept) so I had to go outside, and the baby literally dropped on the ground outside of the shrine.

In order to feed myself and my children, I would sometimes sell produce for others when I was allowed, and I would keep some of the profit to buy food. In 1998 I was liberated by the fetish priest as International Needs had signed a contract with the fetish priest of that village for our release. They had a liberation ceremony and we were free. After my release, my children and I went to the Adidome Training Centre and I learned dressmaking, so that I could support my children and myself. I also received counselling and therapy and a Christian education. I am now an Evangelical Presbyterian. My children live in Accra. Two of them are working and one is in school.

After speaking with Aku, I gave her a gift bag with all kinds of goodies like a stainless steel bowl, hand cream, candies, a mirror, hand towel, pens and paper, soap, toothbrush, etc. She thanked me, smiled broadly and quickly showed it to Patience.

While Aku was speaking to me about being a trokosi, she showed no emotion in her voice, whatsoever. Her story was very "cut and dried." I couldn't draw any more out of her. Most of the answers were just a few words, or she would just tell me parts that weren't too painful to remember. She did however, show lots of emotion and empathy when the half naked woman was hollering on the road, but she had no emotion when she spoke of her own life as a trokosi.

Being a foster parent, I understand when some children come to our home and they sometimes don't react to things that normal children would react to. It is because they have been so abused that they have learned to shut down their own emotions in order to cope. I can imagine that since Aku was only a small child when she was taken from her mother, and then was never shown any affection or love – only abuse - she would have learned not to react, in order to survive.

Aku was wearing a beautiful yellow African print dress that she made herself, and she carried a very small suitcase and a bag of dried corn kernels that she was bringing to her children in Accra. Her other ride was flagged down on the road and as she shook my hand to say good-bye, I quietly slipped 10 cedi (equivalent to ten dollars) into her hand. She was elated! Now her and her children could eat for quite a while. She came back to our vehicle and thanked me again and again, all the while grinning from ear to ear. Other than her education at the Adidome Training Centre, she never had the chance to go to school to learn to read or write. Women and children are empowered by education. When they have the opportunity to attend school, they are taught to stand up for their rights and their freedom, and are given opportunities that they would never have otherwise. It seems like they were never given the chance to speak for themselves. It also seems as though they didn't have strength enough inside to say "no", so others had to (and still have to) speak and fight for their basic human rights..

We were headed back to the training centre for the night. It had been quite a day for me. I had seen and heard things that left me feeling quite drained, even though I wasn't directly involved in their lives. I was tired and glad to be getting back to the guest house where I could have a cold shower and read for a while, before getting some sleep. I found it difficult emotionally, to see how others lived in a different culture where nothing was taken for granted. I felt for the people there and knew that they longed for a better life. Still, they were happy and full of joy (for the most part) with what they had, and they still had hope.

A mother from Kebanu and her little boy with an infected chin

The old fetish priest in Kebanu with his "helper". He was invoking the gods in prayer, while his helper held the bottle of Schnapps.

The young fetish priest Togbe Mama Venornuah whom I
interviewed in the village of Kebanu. He was quite proud
to have the Moose Jaw towel draped over his bare shoulder.

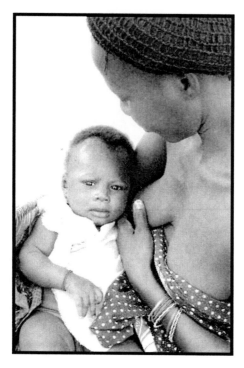

A mother trying to breast feed her baby boy, but the little fellow was more interested in checking out the "white" lady.

Firewood stacked in front of two mud huts in the village of Kebanu

Smoking chunks of charcoal made for fire wood. The prepared charcoal is in the bags on the right. The charcoal is made and sold for income.

Corn "bins" full of dried corn still on the cob. Notice the
goat trying to find shade under the bin.

Laughing school children all clamouring to have their photos taken. They loved to see themselves on the camera.

Liberated Aku standing behind the truck during our interview

The half dressed woman that we met during the interview with Aku. She was so happy to be able to walk away with one cedi, granola bars and some cans of salmon.

The young boy who was driving some cows to greener pastures. He was being used as child labour

Chapter 4

Arianna's Story

January 24th

I *miss my children and hubby today. I didn't think that I would miss the chaos of my home and kids, but I do. Even the snow doesn't seem so bad in lieu of this intense heat.*

I bought souvenirs for some of my family and friends, but need to go back to the African Art Museum to pick up a few more things before I leave. I have been here for a week already, but haven't gotten the interviews that I need for the book. I am not discouraged, a little homesick, maybe. I know that Patience is working hard at trying to get some women to tell me their stories. It'll all work out.

Yesterday when we left Kebanu, we came upon a boy who was perhaps ten or eleven years old. He had about twenty five cows that he was driving off the old dirt road with a stick. We stopped the vehicle and Patience got out to chat with the young fellow, as she was concerned about his wellbeing. She asked him where he was from and where he slept, and if he would like to go to school, etc. Apparently, she found out that he had been brought in from another area and he was working as child labour for someone else. He slept with the cows and drank out of dirty sloughs, and I have no idea what he ate. He probably drank cow's milk as well. A family member would probably bring him some rice or some other meagre bit of food for him to eat every so often, if he was lucky.

He was wearing old cracked up rubber boots that were at least five sizes too large and a woman's nylon shell jacket that was filthy and huge on him. He never smiled, even when I gave him a package of gum, but he took it. I thought about my little foster son living like that, and felt so bad for the boy, living alone with not even anyone to talk to, except for the cows.

It sure didn't look like the cows were fairing too well either. I didn't see any grass worth grazing on, unless they were not stopping in the area to feed. The looked like rather boney cows. While we were chatting with him, some of the school children walked by in their nice clean uniforms. What a contrast that was. The boy had never given much thought to going to school I guess, as it was just not an option for him. He didn't even have that hope. After chatting with him for a while, we went on our way to a school to visit my newly sponsored child, named Kafui.

She was very surprised to meet me and looked petrified at first, until she understood what was going on. She was a tall slim pretty girl of about eleven years of age. She had just started school and didn't have a uniform, as she didn't have a sponsor yet. She managed to "loosen up" a little bit, once we walked to her village to meet the rest of her family, but she was still very quiet and shy. I guess that we were a bit of a novelty there and a dozen or so school children walked with us, so as not to miss out on any action. They all had to get in on the picture taking, and lined up all around Kafui and her family. We didn't stay too long, just long enough to say why we were there and then I gave Kafui a bag of candies, school supplies and a few other little "tid-bits". I did get a letter from her not long after I got back to Canada. She said," My heart was full of joy, when I found out that you were my sponsor." I met her mother and little brother, who was riding in a wrap on his mother's back. Kafui's mother was carrying a load of firewood on her head. They were in great need as they were a very poor family. I am looking forward to getting to know her a bit by writing back and forth.

I heard the African drums coming from across the river again last night. It is really quite eerie. They get very loud and I wonder what is going on. Some of the villages have a real alcohol problem, and I think that probably in their drunken state is when a lot of the abuse towards the trokosis takes place. I am sure it would escalate with the use of alcohol.

I have noticed that anytime we are out driving somewhere, there are a lot of police road blocks. They all seem to have Russian machine guns. There is a bamboo pole acting as a gate that is lifted by the police officer in order to pass through in our vehicle. There hasn't been a problem getting through yet. They just raise the bamboo pole and away we go - no questions asked. I heard that some local people smuggled items from one area to another so that they don't have to pay a tax on those items, and those people are the ones they are looking for. I waved at one of the police guards, and he smiled and waved back. I also managed to snap a picture of one of the guards while he was looking. He didn't seem to mind.

Well, I have been here for a week and I enjoy the African people, but I am starting to get a little homesick when I am all alone in my guest room. I miss our great variety of foods at home. I could sure go for a Teen Burger from our local A & W in Moose Jaw right about now, or maybe some honey garlic wings from our local M & M's. Anything but rice and beans, or plantain and yams would be great. I must say that they have been very hospitable since I have been here, and they are always trying to get me to eat more. Patience even offered to make spaghetti for me. I think that she thought Canadians eat a lot of spaghetti. She sure tried hard to keep me well fed – they all did. I told her that I was just fine and that I had some snacks that I brought along. I just had a pack of instant noodle soup mix a few minutes ago. That was a nice change. I actually find that it is too hot to eat much. The other day I had mentioned that if there was any more fruit leftover, I would eat that. Well, the cook (Eileen) brought me two dinner plates of fancy cut up pineapple, mango, watermelon and papaya. It took me all afternoon to finish it, but it sure was good. The guests are certainly well taken care of, or should I say " guest" as there is only one right now –me.

The girls in the sewing class made me an African outfit from some of the cotton batiks that they had dyed. It was lovely. I only paid about three or four dollars per yard. I went to the sewing class and got them to tie the scarf around my head to get the "whole" African look. I think they were quite happy to see that I was so pleased with their work. One of the students took pictures of me with the sewing class, in my African outfit. Someone said that I looked like an African Queen, and they all laughed.

I shopped in the training centre's little gift shop today and found some nice jewellery, a beaded bowl and some more lovely batik fabrics. The girls in the sewing class have only been here for a week or two so the selection of batiks was not very large, but they were beautiful, none the less.

Patience just came to me and told me that she would have another girl ready for an interview tonight. That sounds good. I will sure need a lot more information if I am going to write any thing other than a pamphlet.

The power is out at times, so that means I have no air conditioner in the guest house when that happens, but I still have my battery operated fan. It doesn't get any cooler than about 25 C. at night here, but during the day it has never been less than 105 degrees F. and that is pretty hot...

"Here comes Patience with the woman I am about to interview. I understand that her name is Arianna."

Arianna's Story

I think that I was around eight years old when I became a trokosi. We didn't keep track of birth dates in our culture. Although I was told what was happening at the time, I was too young to really understand what it all really meant.

Someone in our village had stolen some money, but the alleged perpetrator could not be found, so the offended person went to the fetish priest at the shrine, and asked to have a curse put on the thief's family. I don't know if the thief left the village, or was in hiding or otherwise. The fetish priest took the problem to the god of vengeance and a curse was given. It was believed that the thief belonged to our family, and it was also believed that the curse would bring illness and death. No one really knew for sure, but if

91

someone believed a certain person was responsible (even if they were innocent) they could still have a curse put on the family. Shortly thereafter, members of our extended family were feeling the very real effects of the curse and were falling ill or having all kinds of bad luck.

Family members went to the fetish priest to ask to have the curse lifted so the fetish priest invoked the gods to see how the crime, or sin could be lifted or atoned for. The gods asked for a young virgin girl to serve as a slave to the gods in the shrine, and I was the child chosen - by name - to go and live at the shrine as a slave of the gods.

I had five brothers and five sisters and I was the oldest girl. In order to become a trokosi, many rituals and ceremonies had to be done by the fetish priest to make sure that I was prepared to become a wife of the deities. In one of the ceremonies, all of my clothing was removed while they invoked the gods. My birth name was taken away. I was dressed in the calico wrap (plain white cotton) of a trokosi and a braided rope (the same as the rope that the fetish priest wears) was put around my neck.

As a small child I was not prepared to lose my family and I didn't know that was about to happen. My family loved me, but they had no choice in this matter. If they didn't give me to the shrine, more family members would become ill and die. My distant relatives walked with me to the village of Kebanu where there were two shrines. Another ritualistic ceremony was done there to complete the process of becoming a trokosi. My relatives stole away without my knowing.

Once I realized that they had left without me, and that I was all alone with strangers, I ran after them and jumped into the river thinking that I could swim across, but because I was so young, someone from the village thought that I would drown and pulled me out of the water. My family was gone and I was then told that I would live the rest of my life there as a slave to atone for the sin of a family member. I was full of sadness, but there was nothing I could do, and there was no one who cared for me. I lived with the other trokosis, but I was still alone. I was a small child thrust into a system of brutality.

As trokosis, we couldn't mingle with the rest of the villagers because of the fear of the demonic powers of the gods and the fetish priests. It was the villagers who told their children that to even touch a trokosi would bring evil and death to them and their family, so they avoided us too. I was not allowed to play with the other children. I had to work hard. I was a slave and was allowed no pleasure at all.

The first job given to me as a very young trokosi, was to wake up very early (maybe 3:00 A.M.) a couple of hours before daylight to fetch water from the river. I had to climb down a steep bank and fill a large bowl full of water, then carry it back on my head to the shrine for the fetish priest to be washed in. I had to place his chair in a certain spot and wait for him to awaken, so that I could wash his body for him with the water that I had carried from the river. I was his slave and he was my master and I would have to serve him as he ordered. At times the trokosis would take turns washing the priest and cooking for him. Sometimes, one of us would have to stand over him while he slept and fan the flies off of him. He slept while we stood most of the night shooing flies away and fanning him. When the priest went to brush his teeth, I would have to clean and sweep his room (dirt floor) before he came back. I was a child paying a price for a crime that I didn't commit, and I had no power to choose a different life style. I had no rights. No cared for me and my heart hurt so much.

After the villagers awakened and went about their chores, I would have to go to the fields to work until it was dark, and in these conditions I never had enough food to eat. I was beaten with a cane if I didn't work hard enough, or fast enough. I was beaten and abused for any infraction. As a little child, it was so hard for me. I suffered so much emotionally, mentally and physically. No one loved me – affection was not allowed. I was the ninth trokosi at the shrine, and I was never given a new name. A dog would be given a name, but I was less than a dog. I was just called, "new girl."

The worst part about being a trokosi was the fact that we were always hungry.

The village of Kebanu was a very poor village, so when the villagers got fed, we went hungry. It was so hard to work when I was so hungry, tired, malnourished and sometimes sick as well, but that didn't matter, as a trokosi could be replaced if she died. I had no hope, as I knew that I would live and die as a slave. No basics were given to us. We were not allowed an education, medical attention, rest, or even tenderness. We ate only what we could scrounge together or sneak, but if we were caught eating from the crops, we would get beaten severely. Still, we did what we had to do in order to survive. There was no happiness there, just lots of sadness, loneliness and so much fear all the time. I wanted to have the freedom to choose what I could eat and wear, and I wanted to go to school. I wanted to have the freedom to choose where to go when I wanted, and to live where there was more food. There was nothing to be happy about. The rest of the village got food when they could, but the trokosis would go without.

Sometimes we would not eat for a long time, maybe two or three days. We were deprived of so many things in life and we suffered with malnutrition. There were many forms of abuse. One night after I had come into puberty, I was sleeping when the fetish priest came in, woke me up and forced himself on me. There was nothing I could do. To rape me was his right. He raped me repeatedly and I had a child by him. Then, I was responsible for my child's wellbeing, as well as myself, which was so much harder. The sexual abuse was very degrading, but again I had no choice about anything in life. I took what came my way and learned to live with it in order to survive. I had another child later on, also conceived by rape, again by the fetish priest. The fetish priests did not take responsibility for the children they fathered. The children were shown no affection either. As a trokosi, I was raped whenever it suited the priest, as that was his right. I had no rights as a slave. I could not fight him and I did not ever dream that I would be free some day, even though I was so unhappy. When a girl becomes a trokosi, it is well known that she will be a slave for the rest of her life. I knew that I would live and die in that horrible life.

One day after I had lived at the shrine for many years, we heard that all of the trokosis at Kebanu were going to be liberated. It didn't seem true as when the gods chose a trokosi they were cursed for life. Apparently, International Needs had been talking with the elders and the fetish priests in the village about releasing us, for quite some time. They had been working on a contract that would set us free, and would also compensate the fetish priests for our release. The village was very poor. They had no good drinking water, so many people were ill because of diseased water. The fetish priests had to take this contract to the gods for their approval first, to see if they would be satisfied with our release. It had been agreed that International Needs would pay a monetary price for us. They also said that a

95

well with good drinking water would be put near the village, so they would have some relief from disease. I believe that the shrine was also given some goats and chickens as well. This contract had also been signed by the fetish priests, so they could not go back on their word. There were two fetish priests in the village and they could never again take trokosis for the shrine. If they went back on their word and broke the contract, they knew that they would die at the hands of the gods that they served. This village now has a well, and a school close by with sponsored children in attendance.

Soon all of the trokosis and their children at the village of Kebanu were given a liberation ceremony and set free. That happened about 12 years ago. We were taken with our children to the Adidome Training Centre to learn a trade, and received counseling as well. We were taught to pray and trust God, as we had terrible nightmares and emotional problems after we were freed. We were empowered with an education and with hope for the future. Now I work with the skills that I was taught at the training centre and I can support my children. When I first learned that I was to be liberated I was so excited, because I would no longer be under bondage. I would have my independence. I could make my own choices about what to wear to look good for my children. Their mother would not be a slave and wear the clothing of a trokosi anymore. I could choose my own religion, my own god, and make other choices too that everyone else took for granted. I could choose, because I would be free.

I am happy now, because I am a free woman and no longer under that awful bondage. I am a Pentecostal woman now. I hear the word of God, the preaching, the good news that heals the heart, and I spend time praising and worshipping God.

I am also a married woman now, and have four children who all attend school. My hope for them is that they get a good education so that we can have a better life style and they can look after me when I grow old.

Interviewing Arianna was a real pleasure. She was dressed very nicely and had a confidence about her. She had such a positive outlook on life. She really seemed so full of the joy of the Lord. When she told me that she was a Pentecostal woman, I interrupted her with, "So am I!" I was so excited to hear about how far she had come from the abused slave she had been for so many years to having such hope for the future. She was a beautiful woman, both inside and out. Her face glowed when she told me about how she worshipped God. Her smile was uplifting. She did ask not to be identified in the book as she was afraid that some people might think she was "bad". She wanted to leave her old life behind her.

While pondering Arianna's story about being a trokosi in the village of Kebanu, it hardly seemed possible that the two fetish priests that I had met and interviewed were part and parcel of Arianna's abuse, but they were – no doubt about it. It was all documented. I wondered if the fetish priests had any remorse for what they did to the trokosis, or if they really did believe that what they did, was because the gods ordered them to do those things, including the sexual abuse, as it was considered copulating with the gods. Certainly, it was very convenient for the fetish priests to be able to have sex whenever they had the urge. Is that a way of not taking responsibility for your actions? Is it easier to blame the system, or the gods, for all of the abuse that goes on in these shrines? "I did it, because I was told to, or because I have the power to do whatever I wish." It sounded to me rather like an excuse that a child would give. Then again, if the fetish priests said that they acted on the orders of the gods, were they also coerced by their gods? How much freedom (serving their gods) could they exercise with what they did or chose to do? I do feel that by gratifying oneself sexually, with a child every time one gets the "urge" is pretty pathetic, but then, rape is usually an act of control or rage, as I understand it anyway. Did any of them have any self control whatsoever, or is self control not valued in their position? Were they drunk when they raped? I don't believe that they were for the most part. Others in the village were expected to have some kind of self control – since the fetish priests acted as police officers or judges over the villagers. Maybe they went for instant gratification, as there were no consequences (that we could see) for the fetish priests – who knows?

I did find out that in that last 12 years or so of liberating the trokosis, not one fetish priest has ever come to the saving knowledge of Jesus Christ, even though some of them (including the village of Kebanu) openly allow a pastor to conduct evangelical church services in their villages, even now. They know the very real power of their demonic gods, and I believe that fear keeps the fetish priests in bondage as well. They serve Satan and his angels, and since I didn't want to be chased out of the village of Kebanu by insulting them, I was hoping that the local Ewe pastor (pastor James) was able to talk to them about who Jesus really is, since Pastor James understood their customs, and what would and would not offend them. Until they realize that our heavenly God is above their gods in power and that the battle has already been won, as far as who is actually in charge and on the throne, they will not be able to be liberated from their bondage to the gods that control them. I liked the young priest in particular, but he did believe that their gods were around a lot longer than Jesus had been around. I didn't know if I should have said that in Luke chapter 10 and verse 28, Jesus talked about how he watched (so he must have been in heaven with his father God) as Satan and the angels who cavorted with him were thrown down from heaven "like lightning." I wondered if someone had even tried to explain to Togbe Mama Venornuah, that Jesus has been around since the beginning, but only came to earth two thousand years ago as a man, to be the perfect sacrifice that would atone for the sins of others - for the sins and crimes of the villagers and for Togbe's sins too. The fetish priests are spiritually blinded and foolishly tricked by their wicked gods, who are making innocent children pay for the sins of others. I am sure that the visiting pastor has tried to answer any and all of the fetish priest's questions – if he has any.

Chapter 5

Church at the Training Centre

January 25th

*I*t was Sunday morning and I had heard that the students had their own service in the Chapel at the Adidome Training Centre, and that it was certainly worth going to. I could hear the music and the powerful drumming even before I left my guest room. I grabbed my camera and headed out in a hurry, not wanting to miss anything. The sounds of the singing voices and the joyful rhythm of the drums grabbed the attention of everyone in the area. I noticed that one of the young fellows who was making bricks outside,was singing along with the mesmerizing music coming from the chapel. I am sure that the villagers and the trokosis across the river from the training centre couldn't help but hear and feel the freedom of the music. It was loud, but the voices were full of enthusiasm and joy. What a difference from the eerie drumming and racket that we could hear almost every evening coming from across the Volta River.

I was asked at the last moment if I was going to speak to the girls during the chapel service (as it is the custom for the guests to say something). Actually, I was told – not asked - "You are going to speak to the girls during chapel, right?" It was more of an expectation than a request. I tried not to look too stunned and answered with a quick, "Sure." I offered up a quick silent prayer asking God for wisdom and to speak through me, as I wasn't prepared in the least and didn't have a clue what to say that would have any meaning for them. I wanted to encourage them, but wasn't sure how to go about it.

The singing and dancing was incredibly enthusiastic! I had never seen or heard anything like it. It was similar to the African Children's Choir, but not as rehearsed. After a few notes, most of the one hundred and fifty students got off their benches and started marching up to the front of the chapel, where there weren't any benches. I had wondered why the simple wooden benches were only lined up in the back half of the chapel. Now, I knew. The choir members who were dressed in matching purple African dresses, sang a couple of songs to the rhythm of their drums before the rest of the students joined in. Several of the choir girls beat the drums; their hands a blur in my camera lens. They marched and swayed to the rhythm of the drums and their voices rose and fell according to the melody of the song. They danced in a circle, continuously moving around and around with great smiles on their faces and sleeping babies on their backs, who seemed oblivious to the joyful noise that was going on around them. All of the songs that were sung had melodies that one could dance to. The girls would move up and down in unison as though it had been practiced many times before. One song must have had something about the trumpet of the Lord, as they all moved their fingers as though playing trumpets, while they sang and danced around and around the front of that chapel. Their joy was overflowing in their new found faith, and with the appreciation that they had in being at the training centre. They had hope for their future and it showed immensely in their "joyful noise unto the Lord." Their enthusiasm poured out into all of us. It was contagious. I have never seen dancing before the Lord like that before. I was in awe. Their bodies moved in ways that I am sure would cripple me, but I loved being in the midst of that joy! Their voices were not timid and they all sang beautifully. It was truly amazing! My video clip does not do them justice. You had to be in that presence, to feel it. There was no reservation there. They put their whole heart and soul into their worship.

Between the music, they asked for testimonies. Several of the girls went to the front and in the Ewe language, they told of having terrible nightmares that week, and how God brought them through it, and how they found peace afterwards. The girls that could read would turn to a page in their Bibles and quote the scripture verse that brought comfort to them. While they testified, some would shout, "Amen!" They were in one accord, all encouraging each other – even those who really hadn't yet made a commitment to Christ were enthusiastic when it came to supporting their fellow students.

Pricilla, who was a counselor at the training centre, was a wonderful Christian woman who answered a lot of my questions about culture and anything that came to my mind. She really loved those girls at the school and was so kind to them. I really found her to be warm and gentle. Pricilla explained to me that when the girls first come into contact with Christianity and learn to pray and trust God, they are plagued with horrific nightmares about fetish priests coming after them, snakes, etc. No one pushes

Christianity on them, but they are taught to pray and everything is taught with Christian principals, so that they learn after a while who Jesus really is, and what he can do for them. Before they decide to go from their traditional religion, which involves many gods and the practice of voodoo, they have a transitional period where they need to decide who they want to serve. Most of them are afraid to convert at first so they are not pushed into accepting Christianity. They have to discover it for themselves, and then they decide. I am not positive, but I believe that 96 % of the students become evangelical Christians, and when they relocate to the village or town of their choice (when they have finished their trade school), they choose a church that they want to serve and worship in.

After the testimonies, I was introduced (as though I was someone quite important) which made me a little nervous. I remember reminding God that I was depending on Him, and started by telling the girls how much their amazing music blessed me, and that they certainly knew how to make a joyful noise unto the Lord. They hooted and hollered and shouted, and I told them how blessed they were to be at the training centre, and to that they again clapped and laughed in agreement. I also told them that I heard that even their babies were afraid of me (as a white woman) and told them the story of how when my son was barely walking, a black lady came to our church and wanted to pick him up and hold him, but he was afraid of her too. They giggled over this. I told them how I came to be in Ghana. I made reference to Isaiah 40:31 which says, "But, those who hope in the Lord will renew their strength. They will soar on wings like eagles. They will run and not grow weary. They will walk and not be faint." (TNIV translation) and I tried to say a few more things to try and encourage them, all the while Pastor James translated in

Ewe for the students. I didn't take too long and then sat down and told the Lord that he came through and did a good job –"thank you." I felt that the students were a bit more comfortable with me and maybe some of them would share their story. When the pastor spoke he also referred to Isaiah 40:31 while Pricilla translated in English for me. He encouraged the girls in everything, and while he spoke they would shout out in agreement or clap their hands. He spoke of their future in such a positive way. It was a very enjoyable service and I was so glad that I had the opportunity to be there and share with them. It was all good.

After the service was over, a lot of the women and students warmly shook my hand and thanked me in Ewe. I was touched. No one could leave the chapel until I left first (as the guest), so I quickly got the point and scurried out so that the rest of them could leave and get on with their day.

Sunday afternoon, all of the girls wash their school uniforms and other items, including baby clothing, if they have a child. They use bars of soap that are made at the training centre by the soap making class, and wash everything by hand in small metal tubs or buckets. Once everything has been washed and rinsed, it is hung on a line (there are no clothes pins) or laid out on the grassy areas of the ground to dry. They are very clean about themselves and their children. I saw them bathing their babies in the same metal buckets and then they would hoist them onto their backs and wrap a large piece of fabric around the baby, then tie it above their chest to cradle their little ones.

I was called for lunch which was either rice and beans, or yams and plantain and always a tomato sauce mixed with a sparse amount of veggies and sometimes a wee bit of chicken or smoked fish. The tomato sauce was delicious, but the yam and plantain I think needed to be an acquired taste. The staff was so hospitable to me. They wanted to feed me so much. I was the only guest there and as it is, I don't eat a lot at one time. I am more of a "snacker" and eat little bits all day long. They seemed to want to make sure that I was being well looked after, and I was, but I felt (as the only guest) that I could do more for myself. I am not accustomed to being waited on, but rather am used to waiting on others as a foster, adoptive and biological mother and wife. I wasn't working there and with the heat, I really wasn't hungry at all. As long as I had my bottled water and the odd granola bar and some fruit, I was just fine. The tropical fruit was the best part with regards to the food. I wanted to lose the seven pounds that I had put on during Christmas (and I did lose it in Ghana), and with the heat and not being too active, I didn't want to eat much.

The basic necessities in Ghana are scarce. No one buys a lot of toilet paper (actually, I don't think the locals can afford to buy any) so I figure that it must be a luxury. It probably comes down to a choice between toilet paper or rice, and naturally the rice would win out. I was thankful that my friend advised me to bring some tissues along, as well as some wet naps. I emptied boxes of tissue into large zip lock baggies and took half a dozen containers of wet naps in my suitcase. My hands and feet were always dusty so the wet naps came in very handy. I was told by my friend Ruth, to make sure and carry some tissues in my pockets at all times – just in case nature called out in the middle of nowhere. The guest room had a roll of toilet paper in the bathroom when I arrived, but after I examined it closely I realized that it would not last long. The tube itself was much larger than western rolls with only about an inch or so of actual paper on it, and that being more like paper than the soft tissue that I was used to. I was used to using paper like "Charmin" or other such fluffy stuff. I figured I could manage as I had brought my own supply of tissues. I realized that it was a real expense to keep toilet paper for the guests, so I didn't want to waste anything unnecessarily. I also had to "ask" for more paper when the roll was finished. It was given to me gladly, but just one roll at a time. Before I left to go back home, I had used up all of my facial tissue wiping sweat off my brow and neck, etc. I just don't think that they knew how much we westerners used. Come to think of it, I never saw any plastic wrap or tin foil in the kitchen either. I guess they never had any leftovers. The only things in the guest room kitchen fridge were bottled water, the tin of cookies I brought along (no one realized that I expected everyone else to eat the cookies as I brought them for the staff) and some creamed cheese that we bought at a very expensive grocery store in Accra. I realized that we sure lived the life of luxury at home where we could open our refrigerators any time of the day and grab a yogurt, glass of milk or any variety of snacks. There were lots of tropical fruits that were bought locally for a fraction of what we would pay in Canada. At least they had a fridge (that had to be reset every time the power went out). I noticed that there wasn't a lot of meat eaten in Ghana. It was used mostly for flavour. Very small pieces of chicken or smoked fish would be added to the tomato sauce along with the veggies. I ate well compared to the locals, and I realized that during my stay. The students here are so thankful that they have three meals a day at the training centre. I told Patience that they must feel as though they are in Hollywood while they are here at the school. She had a chuckle at that.

I was watching 4 fellows make bricks here for quite some time today. They were working away quite contentedly with their manual labour jobs in the searing heat, all the while chatting with each other about one thing or another. I noticed that they were painstakingly only making one cement brick at a time. It was driving me nuts! I finally grabbed my camera and decided to go and chat with them about the "slow" brick making process.

They were quite happy to demonstrate their skills and had me take a picture of each step they went through to make a single brick. These bricks were landscaping bricks for the guest room area.

I started by telling them that I was watching them work, and that it seemed as though it was a lot of work to make one single brick. I then asked them if there wasn't a machine that would make several bricks at one time, since they were shoveling a scoop of mix into the mold, it might as well be a larger mold that held at least three bricks. That way it would be three times faster. They thought that was a good question and told me that there was a machine like that in Accra, but that it required electricity. Out here they had to make one at a time because of the lack of electrical power. They couldn't afford to waste electricity if they didn't have to. They thanked me for taking an interest in their work, and they enjoyed the attention and the photographs. I told them that they were working very hard, and I meant it. They were working under the shade of a tree, but I really couldn't notice a difference. It was just plain hot everywhere you went. The "boss" of the brick makers was having a snooze on a bench to get out of the heat. I went back to the guest house and picked up my thermometer along the way. It read 105 degrees F. It was time for another cold shower. The power just went out again, so it was going to be another hot night as well.

I had tried to e-mail home every chance that I had, but with no luck. There was a computer in the eating area of the guest hall but it didn't seem to work at all. A light flashed on and off forever, but the screen never came up. Patience lent me her laptop and I tried using it to send a message home saying that I was doing fine, but we couldn't get enough power to get anywhere, so I finally gave up on that idea. They would just have to believe that I was doing okay. They say that no news is good news. The only thing was that I thought, "what if someone died while I was gone- the funeral would be over before I got back." – kind of a dumb thing to think about, I guess. I thought of Isaac (my littlest foster son, whom I had been mom to since he was only a few weeks old) and hoped that he was doing okay, as he was in the last stages of kidney failure and I was concerned about his health, even though I knew he was in good hands with "Dad."

I was watching some men building an outdoor bread oven with just mud bricks dried by the sun. They were building it beside the fish smoking oven (also an outdoor oven).These ovens are ones that are built for the baking students once they finish their course and integrate into the various villages. Since the towns and villages don't have electricity, an outdoor oven is what is needed to start a baking business. The girls are trained to bake buns and bread as part of the learning process at the school. By the time the oven is finished, it resembles an igloo in shape without the extra doorway. It is a good eight feet high at least and a lot wider than that, and does work well. They have been used for many years, and the way the economy in that area is going they will be used for many more years to come.

The oven used by the girls at the present time was really ingenious. I believe that Patience thought up the original idea. A wooden box made of planks that resembled an old fashioned "wardrobe" was constructed as an indoor oven for the cooking school. They needed something to bake their buns in, and this one really worked. It was lined with aluminum that looked like it was from a roof that had been flattened out as much as possible. Wire racks were constructed as shelves and when the buns rose and needed to be baked, red hot coals (that were kept hot in a square metal container) were placed in the bottom of the wardrobe to preheat the "oven." The trays of buns were then put on the racks and the doors were quickly shut so as not to let out the heat, and rags were stuffed into the cracks of the doors, so again not to let the heat escape. This procedure took an awfully long time and a lot of hot coals were prepared as there were one hundred and fifty students along with some twenty or so babies, and all the staff to feed. To top it off, some villagers would come to visit their children, or the students would go home for a visit, and everyone wanted to take fresh buns home.

They would like to be able to bake more buns in a more efficient manner, so the electrical wiring was put in the cooking area for a commercial oven, but there were no funds with which to purchase even a used bakery oven. Patience told me that she would like to eventually purchase a commercial oven, bread kneading machine and a mill to grind the corn that is grown in the compound garden. For the time being they had to have the mill ground in town and that was costly. I was so impressed with the hard work and diligence of the staff members in trying to make things better for the school. The cost was going to be around $3,000. for a good used commercial oven I believe, but it might as well have been three million dollars, as there was just not that kind of money kicking around. So for now they were baking in the "tin-lined wardrobe" as it worked, but they could not make enough at one time to feed everyone who needed bread.

I notice that the men who were working on the outdoor oven were up to their knees in mud, digging under the earth for soft mud that could be shaped into bricks and then sun dried. This was a different brick making process. They stuffed mud into a mold that held three bricks and then slammed the mold onto the ground to release the bricks in order to dry. It was going to take five or six days to finish the oven and it was quite a project. One of the workers brought his children and wife with him and a couple of little girls latched on to me right away, as I was passing out chewing gum and little metal cars. Again, I couldn't catch their names except for the one English name that most of them seemed to have entangled with their lengthy African names. Mary, who looked like she would be around eight years old, wanted to ask me something for quite some time as she stuck to me like glue. Every question I asked her had a long drawn out "Yes" (which was probably more like an "Ayyyy...)for an answer. She listened quite politely and seemed to look as though she understood.

"Do you go to school?"

"Yes."

"How many people are in your family?"

"Yes."

"How old are you?"

"Yes."

Finally, she got up all of her courage and said four words in perfect English, "Please, give me baby." She was almost begging. I wasn't sure what she wanted and she asked again several times. I finally realized that she wanted a baby doll, thinking that if I had little cars, I might have a

111

doll for her. I didn't, and there were none to be found. Mary walked from the neighboring village, back to the compound several times in the next few days and asked me for that "baby" each time. I finally decided to ask the staff members where I could buy a doll for this child. I found out that none of the towns or villages sold toys at all as they weren't a staple and the locals just couldn't afford to buy toys for their children, so no vendor carried toys. I might be able to buy one in Accra, but wouldn't be going there until I had to catch my flight back home. Because of the language barrier, I asked a couple of the staff members to explain to Mary that I didn't have a doll with me, and no one in the area sold dolls and that I was sorry. The staff members thought that Mary was quite "nervy" asking me (a guest) for a doll and they were going to scold her. I asked them not to scold her as I really would have liked to have given her a doll. They must have said something in Ewe anyway, as she looked embarrassed and walked away. I didn't see her again, but I have since thought that if there was some way I could get a doll to her, I sure would.

Just as it was getting dark outside, I decided to walk over to where the student dormitory was and pass out some glow-in-the-dark bracelets to the girls. I had brought several packages of them along with me, and showed them how to bend them so that they would glow. They were fascinated with them, as they were a never-before-seen item, and they were soon all given out. I tried getting a picture, but all that showed up on the camera screen were the neon bright colours of the bracelets.

I decided to head back to the guest house and turn on the air conditioning and maybe watch a little bit of television if the power was on, but the only thing on the one channel was what looked like a Ghanaian soap opera and the screen was quite snowy at that. They only offered one channel. The soap opera was soon over and Aglow International was on. It was really amazing, as they were celebrating a smooth transition into power for the new President Atta Evans Mills of Ghana. They were announcing that they were giving Ghana back to God. Their Christianity was so open and they were unashamed.

I settled in under my mosquito net to do some reading afterwards, and then settled in for the night. I did notice that in such a malaria infected area, the door on the guest room had several large six inch (or longer) cracks in it where the wood had dried out, which made my room easy access for the malaria infested mosquitoes to enter. I brought bug spray along and also felt quite safe under my mosquito net. I did get nibbled on a bit, but noticed that the skin didn't rise or even itch the way our Canadian mosquito bites did. They just left a very tiny red spot to let me know that they had easy access to my room and had been there. The mosquitoes were also very tiny, more like gnats, but they were so thick that if you were standing outside near a light, when you opened your mouth to speak you would inhale them.

January 26

The power was on, so I left the air conditioning on all night and actually found that it got a little cool so I used one of the quilts that a previous guest had donated to the guest compound, rather than shut off the cold air. I slept much better with the cool of the room. I usually try to conserve energy, but I just can't handle the heat at times. I am soaking wet right down to the skin within a few minutes when I am outside.

I awakened last night to the smell of smoke and for a second I forgot where I was and thought, "Something's burning!" Realizing where I was, I went right back to sleep, as there is quite often the smell of smoke here with all of the outdoor pots and fires on the go.

The time difference of six hours hasn't really affected me here, probably because of the first forty eight hours of travel that I didn't sleep. I imagine that I will have to get used to the difference when I get back home.

I could hear the singing and drums from the chapel again this morning. It was loud, energetic and enthusiastic again and it blessed me. School started in about ten minutes, and singing and prayer started their day.

Pricilla made oatmeal, bread, fruit, eggs and tea, etc. for breakfast this morning. It was enough for a family of four. I ate some oatmeal and half a banana and I was stuffed. I feel rather lazy here as though I am wasting time, when I really need more trokosi stories for the book. That is what I came here to get. I know that Patience has approached the students about giving me their stories, but some of them are a bit wary about being identified and maybe criticized or ostracized by their communities, if it gets found out that their stories are in a book. I can understand that, and will keep some things private to protect them.

Pricilla went over to the school and said that she would be back in ten minutes. It has been close to forty minutes and who knows when she will be back, and that's okay. I wish we would not be as concerned at home about what time it is, as everything and everyone runs according to the clock there. I haven't seen very many people wear a watch here. No one seems to be concerned about time. You arrive when you arrive. No one gets upset when one is late – they just wait. Ghanaians work hard as soon as the sun comes up, and when it gets too hot around noon they take a break to eat and relax for a while. My good friend Ruth would do well here, as she doesn't really pay much attention to the time either. I wish I could be more like that at times. It is hard for me to relax – even now I am getting a bit bored because I am not going constantly, but it is good for me to "wait" at times, although it does make me think of stupid things like, how much thinner the banana skins are here, or the fact that they aren't yellow here when we buy them, but rather green and brownish.

People are also generous if someone needs help of some kind. I have noticed that every time we have gone somewhere in the I.N. vehicle, it is always full, as someone seems to need a ride somewhere and everyone obliges. As long as you can squeeze in, you can be accommodated. In Accra, I saw one van that was so full; the side door couldn't close as someone's "rear end" didn't have room inside the van.

Pricilla returned after an hour or so and took me on another tour of the school classrooms. She has been so gracious and kind. When we entered the classes, they would unanimously stand and say in English, "You are welcome here." I took pictures of the girls and showed them their faces on the camera and they would giggle and poke fun at each other. Most of the dressmaking class had their hair done in various, beautiful braided extensions that were apparently done by the hairdressing students. They would practice on each other. I watched the girls making school uniforms on their non electrical sewing machines. They would spin the wheels on the end of the machine with great skill, and were so proud to show me what they were doing. A couple of them were ironing the uniform pieces with a flat iron that would have been used a hundred years ago. It was a fairly new class of students, but they were going "gung ho" on those uniforms. I gave Gifty (the teacher) the bags of sewing supplies and scissors that the ladies in my quilting guild had donated and they were very happy to have extra snaps, elastic, and other such things that weren't readily available in that area. All the girls were from very poor villages where there was no way to make a living. Educating the girls with a trade would also give them the opportunity to be able to be self employed, thus ensuring a better life style for their families.

After each girl finishes their training, they are given a micro loan, and supplies to get started. They then relocate to a village or town where they believed that they would be able to sustain themselves in the trade of their choice. Several cooking students would have an outdoor mud oven built in a village where several villages might be close by, and they would all share the oven for their own businesses. A weaver would be set up with a loom in her village of choice and also given a micro loan, and so on with each trade that was learned.

The students were going to make an African shirt for Art (my hubby). In trying to explain what size to make the shirt I told the girls that he was a big man. They came back with, "Big, like Reverend Pimpong?" I said, "Yes, that big!" It was rather humorous.

We meandered over to the cooking class and along the way we met Charity and another lady from the kitchen staff, who were rolling up kenkey (keng-kay) for the student's supper. Being very curious by nature, I asked what they were making. I was informed that it was fermented corn meal that would be cooked in a big pot over an open fire. Each kenkey was about the size of a baseball, looked like a dough ball, and was being rolled up in the dried husks of corn (that had been saved for that purpose). It was a real art, and I was mesmerized watching them. The balls were perfectly round and each piece of husk was wrapped around one by one until the kenkey was totally covered. Then the tops of the husks were twisted around until they could be tucked in very carefully. The husks acted as an individual "holder" to keep the corn meal together and would be peeled away before the kenkey was eaten. I was curious about how they tasted, but didn't ask.

A few feet away the beading students were preparing a fire to bake their big bowl of hand made beads. I noticed that there were old bricks in the fire (to keep the heat) and they were using the dried cobs of corn for the firewood. They utilized everything so that nothing from the corn was wasted. Once the fire was hot enough, the beads would be thrown in and then left until the fire was cold, when the students would pick through the ashes, etc. and retrieve them, then they would be ready for the next step (I would assume the painting or decorating of the beads).

We meandered over to the hairdressing class to check it out and noticed that the teacher had her hair in rollers. She was a guinea pig too. Four of the students were working and adding extensions to one girls hair, that way it would only take a couple of hours instead of eight hours with only one student working on the girl. They offered to give me hair extensions too, but I didn't have the nerve to have that done to me. I noticed one sink and only one old hairdryer- probably from the fifties. I don't know if they ever used the old fashioned hair dryer, as I wasn't sure if they even had electricity in that class room, but it was all good. Everyone seemed to be absorbed in what they were learning.

Next, we went to check on the cooking class where about forty students sat in a "U" shape around the table that the teacher was behind. She was stirring a batch of cookie dough and explaining what the consistency should look like. The girls who could write were copying it all down and they were soaking up the instructions like sponges. It was as though they were taking a class in a French pastry chef's kitchen, (on the other hand, it was just as foreign for me to watch the kenkey being made). A few of the students had flat white chef's hats on their heads, while the rest of them had nothing on their heads. The two middle aged widows were also in that class and so grateful and proud to be there. The cookies would be baked in the home made "wardrobe" oven. I couldn't help but notice that it wasn't a very big batch. I am sure they only got a small sample to taste when it was all said and done.

The soap making class was equally as interesting, however, they were making powdered soap that day and I soon understood why they were wearing masks. I only stayed a couple of minutes as I was breathing in powdered soap. I am sure had I stayed any longer, that I could have blown bubbles out of my nose in the shower.

I am a bit disappointed that I have not gotten any more stories from the liberated trokosis. The girls are very shy. Some think that they may be exploited by me. I have been praying that God will open up their hearts so they understand that my intentions are honourable, and they will share with me. They know why I am here, but some of them are afraid to disclose things about the trokosis, the shrines and fetish priests. They can't be forced to disclose anything. They are free and no one wants them to feel coerced or bullied into telling their stories. It must be so hard remembering all the fearful things that happened to them while they were enslaved, when I am sure that they would rather forget the way it was and get on with their lives.

I am a bit lonely tonight. I miss my family. I am the only visitor here at this time and it would be nice to have a real "Canadian" conversation with someone right about now. I don't think I would go away all alone like this again. It would be nice to have someone to share and discuss things with, who is on the same page with regards to culture, etc.

I haven't gotten very many of the interviews yet that I need for the book, and I am running out of time. In my frustration tonight, I did tell God that "this" was just not working out the way I had planned, but had to smile when I was gently reminded that it wasn't my plan, but His. With that, I realized that I had to wait on God and his timing to get what was needed. It took many years for this mission to Africa to come full circle, but it did – in God's timing, so I knew that it would work out before I left for home.

119

Pricilla (a counselor) and the author in front of the nursery at the Adidome Training Center

The author with the sewing students at the training center. The sewing machines are manually operated, as there is no electricity in the classroom.

*Some of the students singing, worshiping and
dancing in the chapel.*

*Pastor James and his little son Casper, visiting with the
author in the guest house. He would hold church services
in at least half a dozen different villages.*

Students at the training center washing their clothes in small metal buckets. They would use bars of soap that were made by other students at the training center.

This was the tin lined wooden "wardrobe" oven that the buns were baked in. Notice the hot coals in the container on the bottom. This was the only way that they were able to bake for the students.

One of the students had to stuff rags into the cracks of the "wardrobe" oven in order to keep enough heat inside to thoroughly bake the buns.

These workers were hired to build an outdoor mud oven that the students would be able to bake bread in. Bricks made of mud were dried in the sun and then piled into a circle to start the oven making process.

123

This is a finished mud oven. These ovens have been used for many years in the local villages, where there is no electricity.

A staff member making kenkey. It is fermented cornmeal rolled in corn husks and boiled. Nothing is wasted.

Chapter 6

The Afrikania Mission

I was awake and up at 6:00 A.M. this morning. It was light outside. Patience was going for a walk to one of the villages close by, and wanted to know if I would like to come along. I grabbed my camera and headed out with her. It was already incredibly hot and Patience was walking at a good clip. We were both quite wet with perspiration within a few minutes. I enjoy walking and could keep up, but I wanted to check out everything along the way and take photos of anything remotely interesting. The dirt road was particularly dusty, as it hadn't rained in a long while. My feet were growing filthier by the minute, but they were washable. I noticed Patience would try to walk a little faster if she saw someone walking ahead of her, so that she could catch up to chat with the person. She always encouraged everyone that she came into contact with, or she had a kind word to say to them. She spoke half a dozen local languages, so that sure helped with communication.

School children were already making their way to school. They were dressed in clean uniforms and many were barefooted as they could not afford to buy a pair of flip-flops. That didn't stop them from attending school though. All of the children by the Adidome Training Centre that went to school were sponsored by someone, as education was too expensive for the average Ghanaian. Many of the children walked for miles to go to school and left very early in the morning. A father passed by with his young son riding on the handle bars of his dad's bicycle. Patience said, "Hello" and told him (for encouragement) that his son would be the next president of Ghana. The father smiled as he thanked her. She would tell the children to study hard as they passed by. She truly was suited to her job, and she was an encourager. Other children were walking to or from the river with huge containers of water on their heads. They were not wearing uniforms, so it was obvious that they were not going to school, as no one had sponsored them. A couple of uniformed children were bickering in Ewe at the town well about who was there first, as they had to carry water home before they could leave for the long walk to school. This was very early in the morning and everyone was "up and at it". Some of the children were going fishing or gathering firewood for their families, as they had to have something to do during the day and besides there was always a lot of work to be done if they wanted to eat that day. There were signs posted in places about children going to school instead of fishing (child labour), but if the family had no money, how could their children attend school? It was all they could do to try and get enough together to be able to eat.

As we got to the village, we passed some bushes where "loofa" sponges were growing. I always thought that they grew in the ocean for some reason, but there they were, right in front of me hanging on the bushes. A beautiful woman dressed in bright clothing was more than happy to pick a few dried ones for me to take home. It was quite interesting for me to see things like that. All I had to do was peel the dried shell off of them.

Patience found out where the chief or head of the village was so that she could go through the customary greeting and arrange to meet some of the liberated trokosis that she knew. She was still trying to get some of them to give me an interview. We spoke to one woman by the name of Alicia, who had twin daughters by the fetish priest while she had been enslaved as a trokosi. We visited with her outside of her home, while she was cooking something in a big pot over an open fire. Alicia had a stand by the side of the road in the village where she lived, where she would sell her cooked foods. She agreed to come to the training centre and talk to me later. That was the best that we could do, as it was market day and most of the other liberated trokosi were at the market selling their wares.

As we walked along, I mentioned the drumming and loud noises that I had heard almost every evening, coming from the other side of the river, and Patience explained again that they were quite hostile over there. They had put guards around the villages, as they did not want anyone interfering with their custom of taking trokosis for their shrines. The fetish priests and villagers knew that on the other side of the Volta River (where the Adidome Training Centre was) all of the Trokosis had been liberated, and they didn't want to liberate their trokosis. They wanted to keep their custom of having sexual slaves, and didn't want the trokosis to overhear anything about being liberated.

Later that evening, Patience asked me if I would like to go across the Volta River to speak with some of the fetish priests. I reminded her that she said they were hostile. She didn't comment on what I just said, but suggested that we could ask them if they wanted to learn a trade. This would have given them something to think about, and the idea of liberating the trokosis would be brought up later. I don't know if my being there would have been an asset to her (since I was a white foreigner and didn't speak Ewe) or if it would have been dangerous. Anyway, there wasn't enough time in the end for us to go. I was relieved at the time, but now I wish that I would have been able to go across the river with Patience.

Again, I was told by Patience that government officials would try to visit the villages to see for themselves whether the fetish priests were keeping slaves, but the fetish priests and elders would not allow the government officials to enter their villages. They would agree to meet them only in areas that were outside of the villages. They would lie to the officials and say that they were not practicing the custom of trokosi. That way the officials could not see for themselves if there were indeed trokosis being held at the shrine of that particular village. The trokosis live in the shrines and no one from outside is allowed to enter a shrine. It is common knowledge that most of the villages with shrines across the Volta River do practice the culture of trokosi. If the government officials could get into the villages and were allowed to talk to the slaves, it would certainly encourage some of them to try and escape, knowing that there was help on the other side of the river. The problem with that is that they would be replaced if they escaped, so that would not help the annihilation of the practice of keeping trokosis. The government officials are well aware of what International Needs has done to help and educate liberated trokosis.

The Afrikania Mission advises the fetish priests not to allow outsiders into their villages, as they are trying to preserve the evil custom of trokosi at all costs, even though slavery in Ghana has been against the law for about 10 years. Apparently (in my opinion) the Afrikania Mission thinks that they are above the law. To this date, no one has ever been prosecuted, even though it is well known that there are close to 30,000 trokosis still serving as slaves in four surrounding African countries. In talking to others (who would rather remain anonymous) I found out that the government officials were actually afraid to enter the villages without permission, to try and physically remove the women and girls who were being held as slaves, as they too believe in the evil power of the fetish priests and their gods, who would put curses on the very same officials and their families, if they interfered. I believe that is why government officials of Benin and Togo have asked International Needs if they would help liberate the trokosis (or voodoosis) in their countries as well.

The problem (as I see it) is that International Needs and other advocate groups could actually go into the villages and seize any trokosis, as they have no fear of the voodoo powers of the fetish priests, but all of the women and children taken would be immediately replaced. That wouldn't be eradicating the problem of slavery at all. They need to reach the hearts, pocket books, or anything else that works of the ones who are the perpetrators in order to stop the practice of trokosi. An agreement needs to be drawn up and a contract needs to be signed by all involved, but that takes co-operation.

Christians who know the power of the one true and living God are not afraid of the demonic power of the fetish priests and the gods that they serve. This last statement would be found to be offensive to some of the Ewe and certainly to the Afrikania Mission who as I understand it, help the fetish priests to continue enslaving little virgin girls. As believers, we understand that any gods other than the one God (Creator of heaven and earth) are false, demonic gods. They are also powerful, but cannot hold a candle to the power of our loving heavenly father. Until the fetish priests and elders can understand that our one God is an all powerful, loving God to all humanity, and who is also capable of empowering mankind with the power of God, which far surpasses their deities, they will not get past their fear of the powers that they have witnessed first hand from their vengeful gods - in actuality, demons.

The spokesperson of the Afrikania Mission has been known to claim that the trokosis are daughters and princess of the divinity, and that the deities will punish anyone who takes liberties with these girls. If they are princesses, why are they not taken care of in a "royal manner"? I have not ever heard of a princess who is starved, beaten and worked to death by the very ones in charge of her. A princess is honoured and treated with great care and respect. What kind of rubbish is this? A princess is spoiled, catered to and does not do any hard labour, and she also has leisure time to do charity work, and represents good and righteous things for the benefit of others. Does "Princess Trokosi" have any spare time? I don't think so! A princess does not do heavy labour for others. She can pick and choose what she desires to do without any fear. A princess has responsibilities, but no one forces a princess to follow their orders. On the contrary, she is the one who is laboured over.

It seems to me that the spokesperson for the Afrikania Mission is calling all of the liberated trokosis liars, as they say exactly the opposite, and since they have been slaves, and now are liberated, I would say that their word is a lot more honest and trustworthy than someone who is in complete denial of everything a trokosi is about. There are too many documented articles about how the trokosis live and are treated. You can believe that they certainly don't live the life of a princess. Does the spokesperson think that the rest of the world is just as ignorant as he/she sounds? I guess that ignorance is bliss in some cases, but with regards to the enslavement of the trokosis, there is no bliss in their ignorance, and they need to know that forcing someone to serve as a slave is a criminal act on the part of the fetish priests and all others involved.

These women need to be empowered by educating them. The Afrikania Mission frowns on education and wants to live in the dark ages forever (or so it sounds) keeping everyone in constant fear of their vengeful gods, where they cannot choose how they want their lives to proceed, for fear of the demonic power of their gods. The old saying that Africa is the "dark continent" seems to ring true with regards to the Afrikania Mission and the way that they think. By educating these women and children, they are empowered, and enlightened, and I think that the spokesperson has a huge problem with that in and of itself. Traditions cannot continue if they interfere with the basic human rights of others. That is where it must stop at all costs.

The Afrikania Mission is an organization who defends to the end, the custom of enslaving trokosis. How evil is it to defend something as horrific as enslaving and abusing little girls and then to lie and say that the trokosis are privileged to be slaves of the gods? The child is not given a choice. They are not even told what is happening during the ceremonies. Where are the human rights of these little girls? In spite of everything written about the evils of the trokosi system, the Afrikania Mission believes that the tradition of keeping trokosis must be preserved, but at whose expense? Are the people associated with the Afrikania Mission so evil, so spiritually blind and self serving that they cannot even recognize that this is an evil act towards their own people?

As I understand it, the Afrikania Mission was started by a Catholic priest who became disgruntled with the Catholic Church and went back to practising the traditional Ewe religion of voodoo and witchcraft, which includes enslaving young virgin girls. Everyone needs human love and security, family and friends. How could any decent person insist that a cultural practice be continued when it oppresses and demeans those enslaved? In the Old Testament (TNIV) Isaiah 1: 16 and 17 it says, "Take your evil deeds out of my sight! Stop doing wrong, learn to do right! Seek justice, encourage the oppressed." If the fetish priests do indeed believe in the God who made heaven and earth, then why not follow his direction to encourage the oppressed – not enslave the oppressed? What is wrong with the traditional religion if they serve and follow orders of gods of vengeance?"

Surely, no one in their right mind would willingly subject themselves to a lifestyle of a slave, with no hope for the future. The consent of a trokosi is never sought. She serves strictly out of fear and she is forced to stay (in the shrine that takes her) under threat of beatings and even death to herself or her family. This system is no better or worse than when the slaves were stolen from Africa and served their white masters in the southern United States two hundred years ago. In the Republic of Ghana, slavery is now illegal and those who continue taking trokosis should be prosecuted to the fullest extent of the law.

What boggles my mind is the fact that the Afrikania Mission seems to enjoy enslaving their own people, and they don't even seem to have any guilt about that, but then Satan doesn't have any guilt about anything either. If no man can serve two masters, how can the Ewe serve many masters - or gods? The practise of enslaving trokosis is immensely disgusting and vile. Those who justify this

132

custom have to be extremely evil, mentally deranged or demonic, as no one who is good can promote the harm of a little child. I have heard that the spokesperson for the Afrikania Mission also has said that the girls at the shrine have a beautiful life. Anyone who has done any research on the lifestyle of the trokosis knows that "having a beautiful life as a slave" is a gross lie to say the least! What former slave in the United States was ever heard to have said that their life as a slave was beautiful!

I am equally as sure that any normal person asked if they would like to volunteer as a slave for the rest of their natural life, knowing that they would be starved, beaten, unloved and abused in many horrific ways would be "nuts" to answer in the affirmative. I heard it said that a spokesperson for the Afrikania Mission denied strongly that the girls sent to the shrines are sexually abused by the fetish priests, yet every single liberated trokosi has said without exception, that the sexual abuse by the fetish priests at the shrine was the worst thing about being trokosis. They were in fact beaten mercilessly if they refused the sexual advances of the fetish priest. The liberated trokosis have stated in fact, that the sexual abuse was very degrading and stole their self worth. So, who then is that foolish spokesperson trying to fool? There is heavily documented evidence that the trokosis are indeed abused in every way possible.

The evidence of the sexual abuse is also seen by the number of children that the trokosis bore to the fetish priests while living at the shrine, and the well founded documentation regarding that, is proof positive that the spokesperson of the Afrikania Mission is a devious liar at best, maybe even related to Satan himself, as Satan is the father of all lies. Does this person think that the rest of the world is gullible enough to believe this distorted rubbish that he is trying to brainwash us with? Any educated person can see through the lies. They aren't even good lies. The truth of the matter is that the trokosis are brainwashed by such fear that they live in a nightmare, especially when the fetish priest takes even their dignity. Once they are liberated they need heavy duty counselling, education and rehabilitation, so that they can heal their hearts and deal with their pain, even though the scars of that awful abuse will still remain as a reminder of what their people and their vengeful gods did to them. It takes years to overcome what they went through emotionally, physically, mentally, spiritually and sexually as trokosis. Sometimes, the pain never goes away. They need to support their children in rehabilitation as well (as the fetish priest takes no responsibility in righting a wrong). Even after they are liberated, the fetish priest does not claim responsibility as their birth father. One would think that if the children were princes and princesses, the father would cherish them even more.

What is wrong with the above picture and the Afrikania Mission to think that they have to sell lies to keep a tradition alive, that is so detrimental to the welfare of these precious and innocent children who are forced and coerced (by fear) into a life of nothing but pain and suffering, and to atone for another person's crime, no less? Not only is that ridiculous, it is insane! I suggest that the criminal take responsibility for his own crime and pay the consequences for the pain and suffering he/she has caused. Shame on the Afrikania Mission, to want to take defenceless children in order to abuse them for the rest of their lives! In my opinion, the spokesperson for the Afrikania Mission must be an ignorant, fear ridden, mentally imbalanced, or demon possessed person to not realize the damage that is being done, and to say that a

formal education isn't important is ridiculous! '....
Afrikania Mission thinks that others are destroying the
Ghanaians "roots" by destroying part of their culture and
religion– taking trokosis.

Educating the people is the key to ending slavery.
These girls living as trokosis lost more than their "roots" by
the sheer brutality of being forced into a life of a slave.
They lost their health through malnutrition, their self worth
through lack of love, their spirit through abandonment by
their families, their strength through slave labour and their
dignity through the lust and the continual brutal degrading
rapes by the fetish priests! I feel that there is a need for
Africans to tell their "own unique stories" to educate others
about the wicked culture of the practice of trokosi and the
evil deeds of their vengeful gods. The people of Ghana
need to hear more painful stories of the liberated trokosis
and their "roots" from living in a shrine. They also need to
hear how the power of a loving God can change their lives
for the better and give them hope for a brighter future. We
need more than just to be "religious".

God, the creator of heaven and earth is all powerful, all
good and he created everything good. He created spirits as
well, but in the history of the Bible it tells us that Lucifer (a
beautiful created angel) was jealous of God, etc. and was
thrown out of heaven with a host of followers as well. They
were fallen spirits and were rebellious towards God, and
God could not have any other take His place. These fallen
spirits are Lucifer (or Satan) and his host of fallen angels
(or demons), who are against our God, the creator of
heaven and earth, and are trying to sabotage the wonderful
plan that God has for each and every one of us. Satan and
his demons are the gods that the traditionalists and the
fetish priests serve, and unfortunately, their eyes have been
blinded by his lies. They (the demons) present themselves

to the fetish priests as other gods of prosperity, fertility, vengeance, and so on. They do know that the battle has already been won with regards to what God has planned, and Satan knows that he has lost the final war. but he is the father of all lies and continues to deceive others.

It is so sad that some people have been spiritually blinded to the fact that God is so good and so full of love that they don't need to have any other lesser gods. I am sure now with this writing, that I have most definitely offended some Ewe people, but in spite of that, I found that most Ghanaians were not liars, but people of honour – unlike the Afrikania Mission and the deceit that they throw out, and stand by.

Liberated trokosis who have now found the one and only loving God through Jesus Christ, know that the gods they once served were unspeakably evil and vile, and have nothing good to say about "the lesser gods" of the shrines. They also have said that they will never turn back to such a wicked religion of idol worship, as they have found real joy in their Christianity. That statement in itself should speak volumes to the Afrikania Mission (if they are even interested in listening to the truth of the liberated trokosis) and what is worth hanging onto, or letting go of. I am assuming once again that they are speaking for the demons that they serve, as they too must be very fearful of their vengeful gods, and that is indeed sad. It is also sad that they are afraid that the brutal custom of trokosis may someday soon be eradicated. Fear makes them lie, and fear of their vengeful lesser gods keeps them in bondage. Little do they realize that they are also slaves of their own fear and slaves of their wicked gods.

There have been no more liberated trokosis in the last five years or so, ever since the Afrikania Mission has

136

started "helping" support the tradition of trokosis by advising the fetish priests and elders not to allow government officials into their villages. The trokosis held captives there do not know that help is just on the other side of the Volta River, so they are afraid to run away. If they are caught they will be returned and beaten severely for trying to escape. No one will help a run-a-way slave (except for International Needs and a few other orgaizations) as there is a harsh penalty for harbouring a slave. The protector will be cursed as well and the curses are very real to them. They have no hope until someone tells them that they can be educated, counselled, loved and cared for. They have no one to tell them, as no one from outside is allowed into the village to speak with them or even see them, so where does one go from here?

I heard of a journalist who tried for weeks in vain, to get into various villages to speak with the trokosis, to try and understand just what was going on in that culture. He was politely given one excuse after another as to why he couldn't take photos or visit with the fetish priests, etc. It was obvious that the Afrikania Mission had gotten to the villagers first and told them not to co-operate. Several times he was told that someone wasn't there, and to come back later, even though he was later told (on the outskirts of the village) that the person was in fact there, but was hiding from him, as he was advised to do so by the Afrikania Mission.

The customs of trokosis and the shrines, are so shrouded in secrecy still in the twenty first century, that anyone who believes in the powers of their gods, seers, physics, fetish priests, voodoo and the Afrikania Mission, will not even help to free the slaves, as they fear the wrath of all involved, as the voodoo curses are very real to them. The journalist's mission to get to the bottom of the practice of trokosi, and go home with a story was very limited as no one would help, because fear ruled the people. I also heard that he had to go through a ceremony to be initiated into a shrine at one point. He was bathed in holy water and was told that he had to bow down before the idols or deities of the shrine to show respect. Even with that, he didn't really get what he had come for. There was too much secrecy and no one would confide in him.

As a Christian, I could not have gone through that ceremony just to see the inside of a shrine. Not because I was afraid to go through it, but I only worship the one true God, and it would have been an act of rebellion on my part and a gross sin and insult to my God, for me to have bowed down to an idle of a demonic god. I would have broken the commandment that says, "Thou shall have no other Gods before me." To me it was just out of the question – not even an option. I was just not interested in compromising my standard. Because of the relationship and trust that International Needs has with some of the villages where the trokosis have been liberated, I was able to get in and speak to the priests and elders, even though they felt that they could not share certain things with me, regarding the shrines and their secrets.

Trokosis are enslaved in several countries of West Africa. The Volta region of Ghana is where some of the trokosis have been liberated, as well as in some shrines of greater Accra (I believe) a city of a population of over four million. Trokosis are also held in bondage in western Nigeria and the countries of Benin and Togo, which border the east side of the Republic of Ghana. No trokosis have ever been liberated in any place other than Ghana. It is estimated that there are close to 30,000 women and children serving as slaves in the above named areas of

Africa. They have no idea that they can be liberated from their horrific life of abuse, terrible suffering and fear.

Chapter 7

Liberated Grace

Last night I had the opportunity to interview two of the students who are attending the Adidome Training Centre. They were both dressmaking students and had only been at the school for a couple of weeks, and were so elated to be given the opportunity to learn a trade.

Violet was a very sweet young lady who appeared to be around 18 years of age. She was very shy and I asked her if she would like to tell me her story spontaneously, or if she would rather that I ask her some questions. She preferred having me ask her what I wanted to know, so that is what I did and was able to piece her story together.

Patience was trying to get her to relax and get comfortable, so she pulled her towards her on the bench and stroked her hair while chatting and telling her how nice she looked. She smiled and soaked up the love and attention like a sponge. Patience had a wonderful way with the girls, and the students loved and trusted her, that I could see. Violet had a problem with her teeth and the training centre was going to have a dentist make some improvements with how they aligned. Everyone affectionately called Patience, "Aunty Pat." It was customary to show respect by calling adults, "Aunty" or "Uncle."

Just before we could start the interview, another young student came up to Aunty Pat with her hand over her mouth, and told Patience in Ewe that she just got her new teeth put in. Apparently, the young lady had only two teeth left in her mouth for some unknown reason, and the school had arranged to have a set of dentures made for her. She was quite pleased to have a mouth full of teeth and giggled nervously while she covered her mouth.

I tried to be sensitive with regards to the questions that I asked Violet as she was so young and shy. After having visited some villages I realized what a huge step this was for each girl who was able to study here at the school. Violet had never gotten an elementary education, so to be able to study for a trade was so exciting to her! She was the first person from her village to have the opportunity to learn a trade. The following is Violet's story.

I was one of seven children born to an enslaved trokosi. I was born out of the rape that was repeatedly done by the fetish priest to my mother. All of my siblings were the product of rape, and the fetish priest took no responsibility for any of us, but my mother loved us very much. The sexual abuse was very hard for my mother, just as it was for all the trokosis who lived at the shrine in our village. I was beaten along with my siblings and mother for any thing that displeased the fetish priest or the elders. I was quite small when we were released, so thankfully I had not yet been sexually abused by the priest or elders of the shrine. This would have been incest, as the fetish priest was actually my father, but it wouldn't have mattered to him, as he refused to take his place as a father to any children he had by raping the trokosis.

All of the children of the trokosis had to go and work in the fields with our mothers, as they were responsible for us and we had to learn from our mothers how to work hard to avoid being beaten. We had to work so very hard, or we would get whipped badly with a thin cane. We knew that if we didn't work hard, we would be punished severely. Sometimes, the fetish priest would give us some food, but most of the time we were very hungry, and so tired and ill as well. We had to somehow find a way to get our own food whenever we could, so that we wouldn't suffer with such hunger. It was hard to get enough food to stay alive, and also to be well enough to do the hard work for the fetish priest.

We were kept segregated from the rest of the villagers, as we were children of trokosis and the villagers thought that our curse would "rub off" on them if they associated with any of us or if they even touched us. The trokosis were slaves, and as children of the trokosis, we were also treated as slaves. If the villagers had food they would not share it with us, even when they knew we had nothing to eat. Many times my mother would only have a small bit of food and she would share it between the younger children and would go without any thing to eat herself.

There was no happiness there – only suffering. Many times when we were so weak and malnourished and too tired or sick to finish our work load, we were severely beaten by the fetish priest. Beating us couldn't make us work harder if we were still sick.

My mother had been a replacement trokosi, taken to appease the gods for a sin that had taken place many years ago. Someone in the family had been accused of having an affair; therefore someone had to appease the god of vengeance. The first girl died at the shrine (probably from neglect and starvation) so my mother had to take her place as a trokosi. If my mother died, then I would have had to take her place, or one of my sisters would have taken her place, but I was still treated like a slave, as the daughter of a trokosi.

One day the fetish priest called all of the trokosis and their children together. We were told that the fetish priest was doing a ritual for a liberation ceremony, and that we would all be set free. International Needs had reached an acceptable agreement with the fetish priest and the gods were satisfied, so after the liberation ceremony we were all free to return back to our villages and see our extended family. My extended family was so very happy to see us all and even happier that we were all liberated forever and the curse was gone. That village is still where my family lives. My mother has a small vegetable patch and sells produce from that, to be able to support the rest of us.

I am the second oldest child and am so happy to be learning these skills here at the training centre. I love to learn about God and His word.

I asked Violet what her feelings were about the Christian religion, and she quickly answered with, "The Bible is going right down into my bones!" We all laughed heartily, and I added that it would get into her heart too. That was a great way to put her feelings into an enthusiastic line.

It was a short interview, but from a little different perspective – being the daughter of a trokosi.

The next story was also from a young girl named Juliet who was about the same age as Violet, also the daughter of a liberated trokosi. Juliet was enjoying her dressmaking class and hoped for a better future with a trade under her belt. She was absolutely, physically beautiful with a wonderful, warm smile and equally as shy as Violet. The interview from Juliet is even shorter, but the story was very similar to Violet's story.

My name is Juliet and I am happy to be here at the training centre to learn a trade.

My story is almost the same as Violet's except for the crime that was done that forced my mother into becoming a trokosi.

In my case a relative had been accused of stealing vegetables from a garden and the angry farmer went to the fetish priest to have a curse put on the thief's family. My mother was chosen by the god's to become a trokosi to pay for the crime of another person when she was only a small child. My mother was also raped and sexually abused, and she also had seven children by the fetish priest, whom he cared nothing about. He certainly did not act as our father. I too, remember the awful starvation, beatings and exhausting work loads that we were beaten for if they weren't done in time. We were all very happy when we were liberated, as we would all be free to make our own choices and we would not be so hungry again.

When I finish my trade I will be given a treadle sewing machine and a micro loan, and I will have my own business, so that I can be successful in my future.

I have not left my traditional religion to accept the Christian religion yet, but I am transitioning. I am learning about God, and the love of Jesus and I am learning to pray.

Christianity is not forced on any of the students. They are encouraged to pray and all the classes are Christ centered. They are taught Bible truths and told how much God loves them and cares for them and that He is there for them, and most of the time by the time they have finished their course of study, they decide to convert to Christianity and want to be baptized. It is a slow process, as the teachers want the girls to know and understand who Jesus is and what God has in store for them. When the girls are released, they need to release their fears and memories, and that takes time and counseling.

When the girls first attend the school and start learning to pray, they quite often have terrible nightmares about the priests, snakes, demons, etc. coming after them. It is hard to

145

leave their traditional religion and they need to feel within themselves that they are making the right decision. Most of the girls need to have their hearts healed before they can make any big changes or decisions. The girls all have counseling and rehabilitation to help them get through the abuse of their past, and to learn how to deal with their future.

Later that day, I had another interview with Grace, who was a liberated trokosi of approximately fifty years old I would guess, but seemed older due to the nature of her harsh life.

She was of small stature, and was missing most of her front teeth on the top. She was rather self conscious about those missing teeth, and usually covered her mouth if she laughed or smiled. She was very open with me with regards to telling me her story, but as usual I had to ask the questions to get the information that I wanted. She was wearing a lovely, dark, semi-sheer dress that she had made, since she had a trade in dressmaking.

Grace was so proud that her daughter was a hairdressing student here at the Adidome Training Centre, and was sure that she would do well. Beatrice came by for a few minutes to have her picture taken with her mother. She was the second generation to attend the training centre, as Grace had become a dressmaker when she was first released from the shrine about ten years ago.

What we need to understand is that even when the students learn a trade and relocate to the village of their choice with a micro loan, it is still hard to make a living, as the general population is usually too impoverished to purchase anything but the basics. For that reason, the students learn several different trades and even then, quite often have to rely on selling vegetables or firewood, when

146

they don't have a customer who requires the services of the trades they have learned. They will also weave mats and baskets, etc. They work very hard to have better living conditions for their families. Here is Grace's story.

I was one of seven children in my family, and I was fortunate to be able to go to school in my village. My birth name meant, "Cherished Child" in the Ewe language. My family and village were typical in the area where we lived. We were all poor, but there was a small school –which would be a thatched roof, mud hut near my village with a few students. (In some of the villages there is someone who has a basic education and they will volunteer to teach the children what they know, even though they are not a licensed teacher.) The Ghanaian people are hungry for education, so they will do what they can to learn, with whatever means is available.

I was in the third level of school, so I would have been around seven or eight years old when I was chosen by the gods to become a trokosi.

It was alleged that a member of my family had a sexual relationship with a trokosi (it wouldn't have been consensual on the part of the trokosi) and because of that, the fetish priest put a curse on my family. No one from the village was allowed to have any contact with a trokosi, as they are property of the fetish priest and the shrine. No one is allowed to even hug or physically touch a trokosi (except for the fetish priest) or show any display of affection.

That act made the fetish priest very angry, as only he could have sex with a trokosi. If someone is found to have raped a trokosi other than the fetish priest or elders, the trokosi must go through a cleansing ceremony, to be made pure for the priests and the gods use again.

When I was a trokosi, if someone accidentally brushed up against me they would shudder, as they thought they would be cursed as well.

My family went to the fetish priest, as our family was having a lot of tragedies, and people were falling ill. They needed to know how the curse could be removed, so the fetish priest invoked the gods, and I was chosen by divine intervention to become a trokosi, to serve as a slave for the rest of my life, because of my relative's sexual crime. No one else would do. I was chosen by name, by the god of vengeance and if my family refused to give me to the shrine, the curse would not be removed and my family members would die. The god of vengeance would see to that. Everyone lived in fear of the power of the gods and the fetish priests. A little virgin girl had to go to the shrine to atone for someone's sin, and I was the girl that the gods had chosen, even though I was innocent and had done nothing wrong.

Many ritualistic ceremonies were done by the fetish priest to prepare me for the gods of the shrine. The ceremonies took many days. During one ritual, all of my clothing was removed from my body and a cloth was put between my legs. They put strings of beads here and there, on different parts of my body. At the shrine I was made to put on the calico (white fabric) of a trokosi, and a braided rope was put around my neck. I was told that I would never be allowed to wear anything else for the rest of my life. Those things identified me as a trokosi, and set me apart from everyone else. I was sent back home temporarily (wearing the identifying trokosi garments) as preparations and resources had to be put together, and there was still a final ceremony to be done. I was allowed to stay with my family for the next ten years until I was about eighteen years old, but things drastically changed in my village after I had become a trokosi at the age of seven or eight.

In those ten years that I was allowed to stay with my family, no one was allowed to touch me, or have anything to do with me. It was taboo. I was forbidden to go back to school as a trokosi, as I was told that I might be contaminated by the others, or else the family curse could rub off on them. I had to wear the trokosi garment, so the villagers recoiled at the thought of their children playing with me. I was never allowed to play with the other children again as they were told that someone would die, and it could be one of them. Other than my family, no one could have anything to do with me or show me any affection. There was so much fear of the trokosis, the fetish priest and the power of the deities, that I was shunned in my own village. It was an awful way to live as a child, but the worst was yet to come.

When I was about eighteen years old, I was supposed to go and live in the shrine, but I adamantly refused to go. My family put so much pressure on me to go. They told me that if I didn't go, I would die, as the gods would see to it. Villagers got together and told me that I had to go back to the shrine as a slave, or it would not go well with the whole village. There was a lot of fear. There was so much pressure on me. I was afraid to go to the shrine, and I was afraid to stay in my village. I was also afraid to escape and run away. Where could I go dressed like a trokosi? Someone would tie me up and drag me back if I was dressed as a trokosi. Eventually, because of the awful stress, pressure, and fear that I was put under, I was coerced into going to live in the shrine, but I was very upset and fearful.

I was one of sixteen other trokosis who lived in the shrine as slaves of the gods. I had to work extremely hard at the shrine. Every morning I had to sweep the whole compound. That meant all the ground (dirt) area of the entire village – and it was done with a short grass broom, by bending at the waist. It was very painful to bend for hours at the waist. No one would help me sweep. It was my job and mine alone, and I had to do it or suffer a terrible beating. After sweeping the compound, I had to work very hard in the fields for the rest of the day. I worked so very hard from early in the morning until very late at night. The trokosis were given one meal a day in that village, but it was very meager. It would be rice, or yam or some cornmeal. There was never any meat or vegetables with it. We were very hungry and tired all of the time, and so we were malnourished and many times we were ill, but we still had to work very hard. If we couldn't keep up we would suffer a terrible beating. Fear kept us there. Sometimes by a stroke of luck we would somehow get a small piece of dried fish, so we would break it up into very tiny pieces and share it amongst ourselves. The other villagers ate better than us.

Because we were trokosis, we were meant to suffer. There were other forms of abuse as well. If I tried to visit my family, I would be beaten. If any of the trokosis would try to run away they would be brought back and would be horribly beaten again. The isolation in itself was abuse. On the rare occasion, a family of another trokosi would bring her something to eat, but there wasn't enough for the rest of us, so sadly we would watch, our stomachs longing for something of substance. My family never came to see me – ever.

I would be badly beaten for any infraction that that the fetish priest was not happy about. It was a terrible existence, but because of fear and tradition, I had no choices in my life. I had to accept it. I was told that I would have to serve as a slave in the shrine for 20 years, in order to atone for the sin of my relative. I suffered so much along with the other trokosis.

I was raped repeatedly by the fetish priest, anytime that he desired to please himself. He believed that his sexual organs were blessed by the gods and when he had sex with a trokosi, we were actually having sex with the gods, so it was okay in his mind to rape me. It wasn't okay for any of the trokosis. It was degrading and humiliating. I had four children by the fetish priest and he didn't care for any of them. My children suffered malnutrition and abuse as well. Even though the fetish priest was the father of my children, because of the deities and the traditional religion, he did not supply them with food, affection or any basics needed. We were not allowed any affection; still I showed affection to my children, as I loved them. I would take them to the fields to work as I had to care for them. They had to learn to work hard to keep from being beaten too. There was no happiness for us there, only pain and suffering.

One day, the priest gathered all of the trokosis and their children together, and had a liberation ceremony to set us all free. Unbeknownst to us, International Needs had been working with the fetish priest of our shrine, on a contract that would set us free. An agreement was reached where the priests said that the gods were satisfied, and they set us free. International Needs purchased our freedom and we were able to go back to our family villages with our children. My family was filled with joy to learn that we would no longer be cursed, because of the liberation ceremony that was performed by the fetish priest. The priest agreed to never take any more trokosis for the shrine. I had served eighteen years suffering as a slave.

I now had no education, no husband to help me, no skills, no job and four children to care for. How could I possibly feed my children? Shortly thereafter, International Needs made arrangements for me to go to the training centre to learn a trade to enable me to care for my children. I was able to learn dressmaking, weaving, and other skills. I was able to support my children at times with those skills, and by growing vegetables in a small garden. Right now I sell corn porridge and vegetables to support myself and my children.

My daughter is in her second year of hairdressing, here at the training centre and my oldest son is in his second year of high school, but it is weighing heavy on my heart, as I have been threatened that if his tuition isn't paid, I will have to remove him from the school. I removed him from the boarding school, but he is still going to day school and he stays with my relatives in a house some ways from the school. They cannot afford to feed him, so I walk several miles everyday to bring him some food to eat. At the boarding school he was getting three meals a day. (She went on to tell me how her brother had started a business and was going to support her son through school, but his business failed, so there was no money now for his education). I am so worried about his education. If he doesn't finish school he will be forced to work as a vendor too.

I am an evangelical Christian now and when I was baptized, I took the name of Grace. Life is hard, but I am much happier as a Christian.

After speaking with Grace, I asked her some questions about how much her son's education was costing and if he was a good student, etc. She told me that it cost $1,050. each year at a boarding school. Apparently, it was only about $300.less expensive if he went to day school, so for the extra $300. a year the students would get three meals a day and a bed, water, etc. There are three semesters so there was approximately $700.left to pay for the rest of the school year. I realized that to be uneducated in Ghana meant a life of poverty, so it seemed like an awful waste of a life to have to drop out of high school if you already made it that far. The amount of $700.might just as well have been seven million dollars, because selling corn porridge and veggies just wasn't going to get that bill paid. I thought, "No wonder so few children get an education in Ghana." It was so expensive.

After some thought about Korku's pending education, we found someone from Canada who was kind enough to pay the balance of Grace's son's schooling for the balance of that year. Grace was elated! She was told that it was a one time gift and there were no promises made for the tuition fees for the following year. She was so overjoyed, that she smiled for the rest of the evening that we were together. It was such a weight off of her shoulders. It was arranged that Korku , which means Wednesday's child, would come to visit the following day.

The next afternoon, when school was finished, a polite young fellow who was well groomed and dressed very neatly came to the Adidome Training Centre. He had walked for miles to keep this appointment. He said his

153

name was Bruce (that was the name he took – Korku was his birth name).

He was rather shy, but very courteous and was so relieved that he could finish his school year, because someone offered to cover the cost. Patience introduced him to me, and he politely shook my hand. She asked him how his grades were and he gave her his marks. He was an above average student. He told us that he wanted to be a journalist, so he enjoyed writing. I liked him. Patience told him that he would have to continue to study hard as a lot of other boys would want this opportunity, so he needed to show how he would work to keep up his grades. He certainly seemed sincere. We chatted for a while and I gave him a gift bag with sunglasses and a cap from Canada, some candy, granola bars, pens, chewing gum, etc. He was quite happy with all the extra goodies and thanked me again, and then he was on his way back to his relative's home, many miles away. He now had some hope for a better future.

A beautiful woman who picked us some "loofa" sponges that were already dried on the plants

This photo looks at the other side of the Volta River where the trokosi are still enslaved. The typical fishing boat is locally owned.

A liberated trokosi and her friend peeling a mound of yams
for the student's dinner at the training center

A child sweeping at the
training compound.

A cooking class at the Adidome Training Center

Four hairdressing students working on one girl's hair

A beautiful young student who was born the daughter of a trokosi

A liberated trokosi and her daughter, who had been conceived through rape by a fetish priest

Chapter 8

The Micro Meetings

January 28th

*I*t is Isaac's twelfth birthday today, and I am not there to celebrate with him.

I am sure Art (my husband) will take him somewhere and get a cake for him. I left his remote control truck hidden in a place where he couldn't find it until this day came. I do miss him.

Today we went on a "business trip" to see how micro loan meetings were held. Patience and two other field workers were going to some of the villages to meet with people who had micro loans from International Needs. We stopped along the way at a place called Sogakope (so-gah-ko-pay) to pick up the two "micro loan" workers from the I.N. field office. "Soga" is the name of a person and "kope" is the word for town in the Ewe language. Lots of towns have "kope" after the name (very similar to us naming a town Georgetown, or Smithtown, etc.)

Before we picked up the two field workers, Patience decided to take me to a village along the way where the fetish priest had released the trokosis from the shrine some years earlier. At that time, he was promised that he would be given a trade and a micro loan as part of the liberation contract. The people were very friendly at that village as well. They all knew Patience, and she was well loved and respected by them. They had at least six looms set up under large areas that were covered in thatching to keep them from the searing African sun. It seemed to be a good situation. A couple of young people were weaving away with great skill. Their fingers and the shuttle were moving at such a rapid speed, it was a blur. They were very happy and proud to demonstrate their skills to us. The priest was not in the area when we arrived, but I was introduced to his mother and took her picture. She seemed very sweet and hospitable, even though she could not even offer us a cup of tea to drink. She just didn't have any. I gave the rest of the stickers and small cars to the children in the village along with a Frisbee. Even the teenaged boys thought the stickers were really special. They were in charge of giving them out.

It was quite a long drive through some decent and some not-so-decent dusty roads. Some of the roads were more like rough trails in the dry season. During the rainy season there were no roads to some of the villages at all. The roads that we were driving on would just disappear with all the rain. We went past several villages and went through several police check points, with no problems again, whatsoever. As long as we were in the vehicle with the air conditioning on, it was cramped, but cooler. Once we got outside, the heat was unbearable again, even when we sat in the shade. I really did not like the feeling of being soaked to the skin for days on end. I found that it was exhausting to be so hot and uncomfortable all the time. Angela and Evelyn kept track of the records for the micro loan businesses (similar to cottage loans).

After a couple of hours, we arrived at the first town where a community industry had been set up with the micro loans. Once everyone realized that the workers were in town, anyone who was involved with the micro loans gathered under the trees of a church yard and parked themselves on roots, stumps and rocks to wait for everyone else to congregate. There were possibly fifteen or twenty women and three men – one of whom was a fetish priest – wearing a bright yellow t-shirt instead of the garb of a priest. I didn't realize that he was a fetish priest until later, or I would have struck up a conversation with him, and put a few lingering questions to him. It took some time for everyone to show up, but one by one they came while the others all waited, relaxing peacefully under the trees, on their chosen seats.

In the meantime, several plastic lawn chairs and an old rickety table were set up for the I.N. workers to conduct the meeting. They carefully put a piece of fabric on the table to dress it up a bit. They took pride in their meeting area. The meeting commenced and each person had their say, once the field workers put their comments in. The fetish priest seemed to have the need to get to the bottom of an issue and discussed at length, whatever it was, in Ewe. Patience, Angelina and Evelyn would jump in very politely as needed and the whole conversation was very courteous and calm. I noticed that no one got impatient or anxious. They just talked until it was settled peacefully. I was quite intrigued with that. I have been in meetings where everyone was agitated and impatient, but I never saw that in the culture of the Ewe people. They were very courteous and polite in any group gathering.

Apparently, the fetish priest could not make his payment that month for one reason or another, and he said that he would pay double the following month, and that seemed to be just fine. They took him at his word and the meeting continued. One by one they came forward with their bank pass books and paid the amount owed or the amount to be deposited into their bank accounts. The money was counted out in the open at the table, while each person waited patiently for their turn. At one point, one of the field workers looked at me and asked if we (in Canada) would count that much money out in the open like that? I answered with, "No, you'd get robbed!" That created a round of laughter.

It was explained to me that the villagers who had micro loans work as a committee to sell their wares. International Needs acts as the go-between to take their products to the market in Accra. Every two months, a meeting is held where the money for the sale of the goods and the payment of the micro loans is exchanged, just like I was witnessing. Each person involved had a bank pass book with picture identification to ensure that their money was going where it should be going. At one point, Angelina took a child's scribbler and waved it in the air telling them that they needed to keep track of their transactions, so that they had records and would know what is going on too. That was in Ewe, but I thought I had figured that conversation out. The actions were clear. It was good advice. It was a good system to help the locals succeed.

The vendors carried their money in plastic or paper bags to the meeting. Some of the women who were dressmakers wore lovely bright coloured African dresses. They carried their babies comfortably on their backs, wrapped in colourful slings.

While that lengthy meeting was going on, I was photographing chickens, wild geckos, and anything else that I found fascinating. The fetish priest noticed that I was taking pictures and asked me to take one of him. His English was quite understandable. I showed him his photo on the camera. He was quite delighted and asked if I would send him one in a frame. I agreed to do that for him, via Patience.

I noticed a fellow riding by, honking a small horn on a bicycle, with a frozen treat cart on the front of it. One of the vendors noticed that he had stopped to see if anyone was interested in purchasing something cold. She walked over and bought a frozen treat from him. I wondered how anything stayed cold in that intense heat, and where he got the frozen treats to begin with. That was a town though, and not a village, so they had a few more conveniences.

In due time and because of all the bottled water I had been consuming in the heat, nature was calling. I was in desperate need to use bathroom facilities of some sort. I never noticed any toilet areas in any of the villages, but we were in a town, so I thought there must be something other than the bushes. I wandered around the church yard and then approached Patience with my dilemma. Apparently, nature was calling her as well, so she took leave of the meeting and we quickly scouted out the area. Close by there was a cement structure about four feet high and eight feet wide, divided in the middle into what appeared to be two washroom stalls. She wanted to check it out first (to make sure that it was suitable for a guest). Patience picked the one stall, and I was to use the other. As I peered into the cement opening, which was only about three feet square, I noticed that there was no toilet of any kind, not even a hole in the ground, but I did notice that the cement floor, which was thoroughly saturated, was slightly slanted on an angle, with a hole for drainage at the lower end. There was no odour like an outhouse, which was nice. I have no idea where the drainage hole took the fluids that were deposited, nor did I care. My only objective was to relieve myself. I was well aware of the fact that anyone could peer into, or over the cement structure, but at that moment I didn't really care. I'd never see them again anyway. Not being used to having to squat, I managed to thoroughly soak my ankles and sandals with warm splattering urine, but the relief I felt was almost instant and left me feeling very relieved. Fortunately, I was carrying the emergency tissues (which my friend Ruth had advised me to do) in the pocket of my caprice pants. I am not usually a "neat freak" but in this case, I felt like I really needed to shower. The best I could manage was to use part of my bottled "with extra- drops- of- Pristine" water to wash off my feet, "dawgs" and my hands, and use a wet nap that I had with me to dry myself off. The deed was done and I lived to tell about it. After that I was determined not to drink a lot if I was out and about, and away from the comforts of the guest house. I could drink all evening in my room if necessary, as a convenient modern flush toilet was only feet away from the bed. I wanted to mention that the washroom facilities in the church yard were well planned. It didn't smell and it took a great deal of labour to erect the walls of cement – short as they were. It was as modern as I was going to get, and it certainly did beat using the bushes.

As soon as the meeting was over, Patience spoke to a liberated trokosi about giving me her story. She would have talked with me except for the fact that it was market day, and she really needed to get back to her business if she was going to make enough money that she needed. The meeting took quite a bite out of the day, so she felt that the rest of the day was needed for her business. I understood, but still didn't have the stories that I needed.

Next, we were off to the bank to make a deposit into the various bank accounts. The vendors did not have a means to get to the bank, as they weren't on every corner and we had to travel to another town to make the transactions. The bank and police station were located in one building side by side. The bank couldn't have been more than twelve feet by twelve feet with only an old desk and a few chairs around it. There was a curtain dividing the front room from the back, and I remember thinking that this was something out of "Green acres" the half hour comedy that was on in the 1960's. I didn't see Arnold the pig, but there were lots of chickens running around outside. I asked one of the two men inside if I could take a picture (the polite way to do things there), and he asked, "Why?" I quickly told him that I was visiting from Canada, and that our banks were "different" and I found theirs interesting. He gave a quick, "Yes" so I just as quickly took one photograph, before he changed his mind. I stepped outside to get a shot of the bank from the front as well. While I waited for the banking business to finish, I sat down on the step and fanned myself with a plastic lid of a container that I had brought some goodies in. I guess that I stood out with my white skin and a fan of sorts. No one else was using a fan.

After sitting there for quite some time, I decided that I would meander around and get some pictures of the local vendors since they were smiling and staring at me anyway - no point in wasting valuable time, when I could be learning something new. Besides, I really enjoyed interacting with the locals and they enjoyed talking with me, even though a lot of it was through body language or gestures. At one point a fetish priest walked by with a royal blue garment over one shoulder and his basket hat. He saw me sitting there, smiled and hollered pleasantly, "Good afternoon!" He waved in a very friendly manner and said, "Welcome, welcome!" and he kept on walking down the road. I waved just as friendly and smiled back. I hadn't seen a fetish

167

priest in blue before, but found out that the colours vary in different shrines. I didn't think fast enough to jump up and ask to take his picture. He may have chatted with me too, and answered some more questions – who knows – he seemed friendly enough.

I noticed a tailor just down the street and he kept smiling at me from a distance. I was a novelty. He had his wife with him and a little boy, so I got up, took some stickers to try and give them to the children along the road on my way to chat with the tailor. The first two little fellows fled through their hut and into the back yard to hang onto their mother, so I went around the hut and into their back yard and showed them the stickers and then stuck one on each arm. They kept pressing them on harder to make sure that they would stay on. The mother smiled, but the little boys weren't too sure what to make of me.

I walked on towards the tailor and gave his little boy a sticker as well. He took it from me and then the tailor started to chat with me. Both he and his wife had broad smiles on their faces. Their little boy was pretty serious while he stared at me and listened to my odd language. I remarked about his business and he was quite proud of his old treadle sewing machine, especially after I told him I had one just like it that had belonged to my grandmother. I also told him that I did dressmaking for years. Well, we were on the same page then. He smiled and introduced me to his brother who was sitting in the next booth. He made drums and they were over five feet tall. He proudly posed for a picture beside his drums that he had leaning against the wall.

I sauntered back towards the bank only to find that they were still occupied, so I decided to have a chat with the police officer who was sitting on a chair at a table, which was just in front of the open police door. He was very friendly after I started the conversation, but reserved. I asked him if he would like to look at my photos of my family in Canada and he was more than willing to see where I was from. He looked at each picture and was very intrigued, as he held my small album, while I explained who was in the photographs. He looked at the ones with the snow and at our home covered in snow, my children, family, etc. and was fascinated. I don't think a visitor ever thought about sharing pictures with a police officer there before. He was very polite and thanked me for sharing those with him, and I said something complimentary about Ghana and then I sat back down on the steps outside of the bank, fanned myself some more and waited. I found out afterwards that even most police officers don't know what trokosis are, and that there is even a law against slavery. Some do, but since it so closely guarded and secretive, even a majority of Ghanaians don't know that there is such a thing as slavery in the small villages and some of the towns. Emanuel, the taxi driver in Accra didn't know what I was talking about when I asked him what he knew about the ancient culture of trokosis.

It wasn't too much longer and they were finished. In the meantime a friendly gentleman came by and asked who owned the vehicle. I said, "International Needs" and he proceeded to thank me for everything that International Needs was doing for Ghanaians. I finally figured out that I couldn't explain why "I" was there, so just thanked him and he went on his way. It made him feel good to thank a team member, and so I didn't have the heart to let him think I really wasn't one, and have him be embarrassed about all the nice things he said about International Needs. I realized how Ghanaians appreciated International Needs *and what trust they had in the organization. I was glad I was writing the book on their behalf.*

We had one more meeting to attend and it wasn't too far away, so we all got aboard and drove to another smaller village, or at least a smaller committee of micro loan customers. At this place, a retired teacher was the spokesperson for the group. It wasn't a very long meeting this time, as there were only a few women – maybe six at the most. A young girl came by selling shelled roasted peanuts, bags of water and bananas. We bought some of each. The peanuts were very fresh as they were grown there, and of course the bananas were equally as fresh. The bags of drinking water sold for five pesos each and they would bite a tiny hole in one corner and then suck the water out. I chose to continue drinking out of the litre bottles, as I am sure I would have spilled the bag of water all over the front of me. The bags were incredibly flimsy and thin – kind of like a bag from the supermarket that you would put your veggies in. Once they finished drinking, the bags were dumped unceremoniously on the ground to be downtrodden by anyone who walked in that direction, and no one noticed.

This was the last meeting for the day and it was too late to go back to the bank, so that suited me just fine.

We were finally heading back to the guest house. It had been a long day for everyone. We did stop along the way where a vendor wearing an American "rock" shirt was selling fruit by the side of the road, so we bought three pineapples and two papayas for a total of one cedi ($1.00 Canadian). It was just getting dark when we got back to the training centre. Pricilla was preparing something for us to eat and when we were all called for dinner an hour later, we were good and hungry. A woman sat down beside me in *the dimly lit dining room without saying anything. I decided to introduce myself to her, only to find out that it was Evelyn. I was so embarrassed, and I am sure that she thought I was a little "nutty." She had gotten cleaned up and instead of wearing jeans she had on a colourful cotton dress, and where her hair had been in a bun, it was now falling around her shoulders, so I hadn't recognized her in the darkened room. I got over it, and I am sure she did too.*

Later that evening I was sure that I heard rain, and it was coming down "big time." I went outside only to discover that it wasn't raining at all. I went back into my guest room and heard the rain again. I was sure that it had to be coming down on the tin roof, but again I checked and there was no rain. Then I got a whiff of that smell again – smoke! Something was on fire. Something was always on fire there with the ovens, smoking of fish, outdoor cooking, etc.

I walked out farther onto the yard, then turned around and saw billows of thick smoke coming out over the back of the quest house where I was staying. I got a little nervous and thought that I must check this out. I had my passport and ticket in my money belt, so was ready for any emergency, or so I thought.

As I walked to the side of the guest house kitchen area, I saw what appeared to be an out of control bush fire. It was crackling and burning up the dried weeds and grasses, and I could see that it was spreading rapidly. Naturally, I started snapping pictures and taking some video as well. The new cook was standing outside behind the guest kitchen, looking a little concerned. I looked towards the school area and saw some of the students watching the" blazing inferno."

Having lived on a farm, I knew that the fields were sometimes burned purposefully, but not when the weather was dry, as it would be too dangerous and could get out of control. I saw the security guard, who was also the gardener and handyman, just resting on the edge of the building with his hands behind his back, and looking very relaxed. He was watching the bush fire, with what seemed like no concern whatsoever. He really only knew a few words of English, so with all the hand gestures and body language, I assumed that he had set it for some reason, but why? The new cook finally figured out that it was just a random bush fire that started on its own.

They seem to have a lot of bush fires in the dry season, but they burn themselves out usually without doing any damage. Fortunately, the wind was blowing away from the compound; it wouldn't catch any of the buildings on fire. It was a windy evening, and we could hear the crackling of the ever so dry brush in the open field, but only the dry brush was burning. After an hour or so, it stopped burning, much to my relief.

The women of the micro loan meeting sitting on stumps or anything else that they found comfortable.

The three men who were part of the micro loan meeting. The fellow on the right was a fetish priest who had liberated the trokosis in his village. He was very friendly and likable.

173

This was the toilet facilities that we used near the micro loan meeting site. It was in a church yard and was built for the congregation.

The police station and the bank, where the International Needs workers made the deposits.

174

The tailor, his wife and child.

Chapter 9

Two Trokosi Stories

Last evening, I was asked to come and sit in the guest gazebo, as Alicia had come and wished to share her story with me about her life as a trokosi. I immediately grabbed my audio recorder, pen and book, a gift bag and my camera and after spraying heavily with bug spray, I walked out to meet her.

She was dressed in a lovely denim skirt with fringes, so I assumed she had a trade as a dressmaker. She was proud of how she looked. She had a glow about her that told a story of a thousand words. She looked happy. I asked her if she had made her skirt and she said that she hadn't, but seemed proud and complimented that we noticed it.

Patience knew Alicia, but tonight was special as Alicia had asked if Patience would like to go to a service at her church, after we were finished the interview. It came as a surprise and she was delighted that she had been asked. We had to get started as Alicia didn't want to miss the service, or be late. Here is Alicia's story.

I remember my life as a child, before I was forced out of fear to become a trokosi.

There were ten children in my family and I was the fourth. I was expected to do chores as part of a large family, but I could run and play with the other children of the village after my work was done. Sometimes we didn't have a lot of food during certain seasons, but we ate the same as the rest of the villagers. Life wasn't always easy, but I was a happy child living with my family, and I knew that they loved me.

My father was not very careful (or moral) and he would have sexual affairs with some of the other women in the village and children were born because of it. He had been warned to stop his bad behaviour, but he didn't heed the warning, so an angry person went to the fetish priest and asked to have a curse put on our family. I don't know why the curse is put on the whole family, instead of just the guilty person. The fetish priest took the complaint and invoked the god of vengeance to have revenge, thus our family was cursed. Family members were becoming ill and we were afraid that they would die. My family asked the fetish priest what we could do to have the curse removed. Again the gods were invoked and it was demanded of the gods that a young virgin girl would have to become a trokosi, to atone for the sins of my father, in order to have the curse lifted.

I was about nine years old when it was predicted by the gods that I was to become a trokosi, to serve a life as a slave in the shrine, but no one told me that I was to become "the" trokosi. There were many traditional ceremonies that were performed by the fetish priest, in order to prepare me for service to the gods.

In one particular ceremony, my clothing was stripped off my body and I was dressed in the white wrap of a trokosi. The rope was place around my neck, so that I would be identified as a slave. I didn't understand at that age what was happening. No one explained anything to me. Everything was secretive. The adults knew what was happening, but I believe that it was kept from the children on purpose, as the child may run away if they had any knowledge that all the ceremonies were in preparation to prepare them to live the life of a trokosi. If I or other girls knew in advance, we might try to escape. My birth name was also stripped from me. I was stripped of my clothing and my name, and had no idea that I would soon be stripped of my dignity and basic human rights as well.

After the week long ritualistic ceremonies were over, I was told that I must go with my relatives in a boat across the river, so I complied. That was where the shrine was that I was to live in, but I still knew nothing. No one in my village wore the identifying clothing of a trokosi. In the morning, when my family went back to the river to go home, I naturally followed them back to the rivers edge. It was then that they informed me that I could not go home with them, and that I was to live in the shrine with the other trokosis to atone for the sins of my father. I did understand that a trokosi was a slave as they had been talked about in the village, but we did not have a shrine in our village and needless to say, I was devastated and heartbroken that my family just left me there. I realized that I had been abandoned and sat by the edge of the river and cried all day. No one from that village cared or even seemed to notice that I was crying. Finally, when it was dark, someone from the shrine came to get me, and my life of suffering as a slave began.

A trokosi is not allowed any affection. If someone touched a trokosi, they were afraid that they would be cursed too. I was isolated from the rest of the villagers – even the children. I could only be in the company of the other slaves. We were not included in any of the festive village celebrations. There were about twenty five trokosis living in that shrine. I was given the chore of having to wake up at 4:00 A.M. each morning before anyone else was up, to perform a ritualistic cleaning and sweeping around the gods (idols) in the shrine. Once I was finished with that, the other villagers were just getting up at dawn. I was expected to follow them to the fields to work very hard until about 2:00 in the afternoon. When we came back to the village from the fields, I was to go fishing until it was too dark to fish any more, so my life was just work, work, and work as a child of only nine.

I was not allowed to play at all. If I played, it meant that I was being disobedient and I would be punished. If there was a little bit of time left between jobs, I would have to sit quietly by myself and just look on until I was directed or ordered to do something else. I couldn't jump or run or move too much. I had no happy times there. I was controlled by terrible fear. We feared the deities and death and illness. We feared the fetish priests and elders. We feared the demonic powers around us. We lived with fear, pain, suffering, starvation and more. We didn't know about a God of love. We only knew fear and pain. We had to stay there to serve the gods and deities, or we were told that we would die and our families would suffer too. I was very depressed and fearful as a little child and the whole time that I was a trokosi. My life was without any hope whatsoever. Just to be able to get enough food to eat was difficult. The rest of the villagers didn't go hungry, as they had fields of vegetables and when you are free, you can provide for yourself and your family. We were told that if we stole food from the fields, we would die. I was not free, and trokosis have no access to anything, including food. Many times I went all day with nothing to eat and sometimes was too weak to work, but I would be beaten severely with a thin bamboo cane that was like a whip, if I was not able to finish my work load. At other times, I would have to kneel for hours on sharp, broken, chards of shell (Alicia lifted her skirt to show me the large ugly scars below her knees) with no medical attention afterwards. There were other torturous punishments as well for small infractions or sometimes for what was nothing. The fetish priest delighted in seeing us suffer. Sometimes I would have to put the tip of one finger on the ground and lift one leg up in the air and I would have to stay in that position until I was so exhausted, I would cry out in pain. There was so much abuse and I couldn't escape it. I didn't know that I had any human rights. Trokosis are not aware of anything outside of what they are required to do. We are not even given any news or any information. We are kept in the dark. When I became ill, I would be given boiled herbs to drink, as it didn't matter if I lived or died, because I could and would be replaced with another innocent, little virgin girl. I was sexually abused by the fetish priest as it was his right. He claimed that I was also a "wife" of the gods. We had to perform ritualistic sexual acts in the shrine, as trokosis, but these are not talked about as they are secretive. They were horrible, evil rituals.

I had tried to run away, but was forcefully brought back. I was then beaten for trying to escape. There was so much abuse that I couldn't ever escape it. I finally just gave up trying to help myself and the abuse continued. There is a heavy fine imposed on anyone who protects or harbors a trokosi, so even relatives will return a trokosi to the shrine.

They are so afraid of the demonic power of the fetish priest, and of the deities and idols themselves. I was thankful that even though I was raped continuously by the fetish priest, I did not have a child by him, while I lived at the shrine. I could not feed myself properly, let alone care for a child. Some trokosis had as many as ten or fifteen children by the priest and then had no help with supporting and feeding them. Their children were abused as well. I spent fifteen years suffering as a slave of the gods, because of the sins of my father.

When I found out that I was going to be liberated, I was so happy. I never had hope that this day would ever come. I believed that I would die at the shrine. International Needs had in fact bought our freedom by having the fetish priest sign a contract. There was an exchange of money and other things to pay for our liberation, and a ceremony was paid for so that the fetish priest could invoke the gods to allow us to go free. At last the gods were satisfied with the arrangements that had been made, and the contract was signed that stated the fetish priest could no longer take any more trokosis for the shrine.

I went back to my family and we were all very happy and filled with joy that the curse was broken and I was free at last. They believed that I was free only because the liberation ceremony had been done by the priest, otherwise I could not have gone back home, because of my families fear.

After all the mental, physical, sexual and emotional abuse that I suffered, the worst memory was that of being abandoned by my family, when I cried all day by the edge of the river. My spirit had been broken that day and it still haunts me. I kept asking questions back then, but there were no answers. The experience of living as a trokosi still lives with me.

Once I was released, I went to the Adidome Training Centre and learned a trade in hairdressing and some other skills. I learned about the love of the one true living God and I received counseling and rehabilitation, so that I could realize my worth as a woman and a child of God. I chose the name of Alicia when I was baptized into the Christian faith and gave up the traditional religion that had done nothing for me that was positive, good or kind. The traditional Ewe religion only brought me pain.

I do hairdressing to support my twin daughters and I also have a vending stand where I sell kenkey and other food items. My daughters help me when they are home from school.

The best thing about being free is being in the house of the Lord and worshipping. We sing and clap and dance. My new God gives me hope for the future.

After Alicia finished her story, Patience and I went with her to her church for a service. Now, in her liberated state, Alicia was a princess – a child of God. The music was inspiring and the dancing was exuberant. Little children played the instruments along with the older musicians. The smaller girls slapped some kind of rhythmic gourds that had been loosely covered with shells. They would dance and sing while they rhythmically whacked those shells. It was good to see those little children involved in the service. I tried to picture them as trokosis, and thought how sad that would be compared to their lives right now. They were filled with joy to know God and feel his presence at such a tender young age.

On days when there hadn't been too much to do or places to go, I would walk along the dusty roads in either direction just to visit with the locals. There was nothing to be afraid of. No one would try to rob me or take my camera, etc. They had too much self respect for that. I saw a lot of termite hills and soldier ant hills that were all of fifteen feet high. I chatted with a family who was collecting firewood at the side of the road. I spoke with another gentleman who told me that a certain tree that looked like it had large cotton balls on it that were used to make pillows.

One time someone told me about the huge tree in the middle of the town called the baobab tree which had an enormous bottom and thick trunk, with little branches and leaves. It looked out of proportion. Apparently when it was the dry season, elephants would break off the small branches and put their trunks into the tree cavity and drink from the water reserved inside.

One village that we walked to had so many children wanting their pictures taken. They were delightfully refreshing. I gave Patience five cedi at a candy vendor's stand so that each child could have some candy. Some of them had never had candy before, unless they received a Christmas shoebox from N. America.

We had walked through Alicia's village a couple of times that week, and on the last walk I saw one of her daughters selling food at the vending stand. She had made peanut soup and there was warm kenkey ready to eat. I thought that I would like to try some of the kenkey before leaving for home, so for ninety pesos (less than a dollar) I bought three of them to take back to the compound for one of our meals that day. One of the kitchen staff warmed them up with some of the customary tomato sauce mixed with a few veggies, and I was ready to give it a try. I took just a small amount of Kenkey on my plate, as I wasn't sure whether or not I would enjoy it. I had liked (and eaten) everything else that I had been served, but since I paid for the kenkey, I wouldn't feel bad by wasting it, if I thought it just wasn't palatable. I tried it without the tomato sauce at first, and it was vile! It was sour and fermented – on purpose apparently. I think that maybe as the old corn starts to ferment, they make kenkey, so as not to have the rest of the corn crop wasted. I tried it with the sauce and it was equally as vile tasting. No offence to the chef, but I just couldn't even swallow it. Patience ate away at it. I think it had to be something that you acquired a taste for, and I just wasn't going to live long enough to acquire a taste for kenkey.

Earlier yesterday we were at the village where Alicia lived with her girls. We also were able to speak with Faith who also had been a trokosi for many years. She wept while she shared with us. It was very difficult and emotional for her to talk about her memories as a slave. I felt awful for having made her relive it all again. Patience tried to counsel her through it, and we had to pause from time to time so that Patience could tell her that the more she talked about it, the easier it would get. Patience was so kind to her, and so trusted by everyone she knew. Eventually, we were able to get the interview, while her newborn infant slept inside her mud house; she cradled her sick toddler in her arms as she spoke. The little girl was not feeling well. I was able to meet Faith's husband during the interview. He worked every chance that he got at whatever he could find, but they were struggling to get by. It took a while to clear the courtyard so that Faith had enough privacy to share with us. Everyone wants to visit if there is a guest. Patience brought her a bucket of bars of soap to help out. Faith's story which follows was equally as hard to listen to, as it was for her to tell it.

I was chosen by the deities to be a trokosi when I was around the age of ten. It was alleged that someone in my family had an affair with a trokosi at the shrine in my village. Someone in the village was very upset with him – it could have been the fetish priest as the trokosis were his property – so a curse was put on my family by the fetish priest, through the powers of the deities. In order to have the curse removed, a young virgin girl had to be sent to the shrine to atone for the sin of the relative. The gods chose me to become a trokosi or "wife of the gods" to appease the deities. Even though I was so young and innocent, I had to pay for his crime, yet I had done nothing wrong.

No one told me what was happening when I had to be involved in a lot of rituals and ceremonies for many days. At first, because I didn't understand what was happening, it didn't mean much to me, but when I found out that I was going to be sent to live at the shrine as a trokosi, I was very angry and upset as I didn't want to be a slave! Who would want to be a slave of the gods? I was just a little girl.

The shrine that I was going to live at was in our own village, so I was forced to be a slave in my own village where my family lived, and there was nothing that I or my family could do about it. If they refused to give me to the shrine, they would fall ill and die, and so would I.

I had nothing to be happy about after I became a trokosi. I suffered so much in my own village. I was isolated from my former friends and the other children in the village that I used to play with. I was not allowed to be a part of the village affairs anymore, and I had no opportunity to attend school. I only knew hard work, pain and suffering. My family did not even supply me with food at the shrine, although I lived in the same village as them. I had to look after myself. I would collect firewood and sell it when I had the chance, to get enough food to eat. Even then, I was always hungry. Sometimes I would make charcoal to sell if I had any extra time.

I had to work very hard and carry loads that were much too heavy for a child my size. I was small for a ten year old. As a slave I could not refuse to do the work that the fetish priest ordered me to do, because of the fear of beatings and other punishments. I would gather thatching in the bushes and carry the heavy bundles back to the village for roofing. Many times I would be loaned out as labour by the fetish priest, to do other peoples hard work so that he would benefit from my hard work as a trokosi child.

No one could show me any tenderness as a trokosi. I was not allowed to be touched or hugged. When I was sick, I was not allowed to go to the hospital as there was no money to care for a trokosi. I would be given some herbs to drink and if it didn't make me well, it didn't matter anyway, so – good luck – I could be replaced by another little virgin girl if I died.

Sometimes when there was no food, I would have to beg for the children of the other trokosis and myself. I was so malnourished and always suffering from hunger, pain, humiliation and despair. So many times when there was no food, the trokosis would go to the fields and pick some red hot peppers that had dried on the ground. We would grind them up and then eat them, so that we would have to drink lots of water to feel full. They were painful to eat like that as they were so hot and spicy. Even our children had to eat them to keep from having such awful hunger pains. We would force them down their throats so that they would drink more water. The hot peppers made us drink so much water. No one wanted to eat the hot peppers, but we were forced to, or we would have died of dehydration. I was a slave in every sense of the way and had to appease the gods of vengeance. It is very hard for me to tell this as I relive it every time I talk about it (at this point she was sobbing and Patience had to step in to counsel her for a few minutes - she continued again....).

When people would arrive in our town and need someone to help carry heavy loads and to work very hard, they would talk to the fetish priest and strike up a bargain, and we would be used as beasts for hard labour. There were twenty four trokosis living in that shrine with their children. When one of them would die, she would be replaced with another little girl, and sometimes it was a child of the dead trokosi. Sometimes the crime was committed so long ago that no one even remembered what the crime was, but that didn't matter as long as a little girl could be kept in slavery.

If the work was too hard and I couldn't physically do it, I would be beaten badly. If I refused to work I would be whipped and also for any time that I displeased the fetish priest, I would again be beaten with a thin bamboo cane like a whip. I was raped repeatedly by the priest and had a child by him, but the priest didn't care about his child. I had no choice in the rape. I would be beaten if I didn't comply with his perverted sexual demands. If I was supposed to be copulating with the gods through the fetish priest, you would think that my child would be valued by the gods, but the gods they served were cruel. It was so much harder then, to have to raise and care for my child as well as myself.

I lived in so much fear – fear of when the fetish priest would come at night to rape me when he wanted to fulfill his lust. I lived in fear of punishment, beatings, hunger, humiliation, rape and death. I never had any hope that I would be free. I thought that if I went free, my family and I would suffer even more and then die. I was a slave to be used in any way the fetish priest and the gods desired. The fetish priest put such fear in the trokosis with his demonic power, that we believed if we didn't comply with his demands, we would die, so we did what we had to do to try and survive with as little suffering and punishment as we had to bear.

We were not allowed to take food from the gardens and we were not able to have a little garden to feed ourselves with. We had to work the fields of the fetish priest and others as well. We had no rights and didn't realize that our human rights were being violated. We were kept in such isolation that we did only what we were ordered to do in order to survive. I served seventeen years as a trokosi and was never shown any affection. I have no happy memories of life as a trokosi. The only memories I have are of pain and suffering and degradation. (By this time she was sobbing again…we stopped….Patience counseled her, and then she continued again…)

When my name was taken from me at age ten, I was not given another trokosi name but was just called MaMa (not as in mother), but it sounded like Mu Muh with the accent at the end. It is not a name at all, but a title like, "slave" or "worker."

When I found out that we were going to be liberated and be set free I had joy – so much joy! I could hardly believe it was true! The villagers taunted us when they found out that we were to be liberated, as they said it was not possible to undo what was done by the gods. They told us that we were still cursed, even after the fetish priest performed the liberation ceremony. They were not happy for us, as they were still afraid of the curses.

After I was set free I was so happy! There were choices that I could make. I could wear what I wanted to wear to look beautiful, and I could choose where I wanted to live and work. No one ordered me around or told me what to do. I was a free woman! I did things that brought me joy.

Finally, after a while the villagers were happy too and they shared my joy. They realized that if they touched me they would not be cursed. Soon after, I went to the Adidome Training Centre to go to school and I learned all kinds of skills to be able to live and support my daughter. I did go through counseling, but it is still hard to remember the bad days that are part of my past. I am married now with two small children (and I have an older daughter conceived through rape by the fetish priest) and it is so hard to get ahead in life. My husband finds work whenever he can. Life is difficult, but so much better as a free woman. I chose my name when I was baptized as a Christian. I am an evangelical now. I have hope that my children can go to school and get an education. People here don't think we have much as we live in this house (her house was not very nice) but we do have hope, because God is good and He will help.

Faith's story was especially hard to listen to. She was very emotional as the wounds were still there after many years. It sometimes takes a very long time to recover from such awful abuse, and for just the scars to remain. It sometimes never really goes away. She was also recovering from having just delivered a baby, so she was very tired too. I didn't think I could listen to any more trokosis stories. Everyone's story was basically the same. Each story was filled with abuse, degradation, fear, isolation, rape, etc. etc, but in the end, – hope. How many trokosis who are still enslaved have hope? None of them, as they cannot be reached – they are isolated.

The problem lies in the fact that the government officials are too afraid to actually go into the shrines and remove the women and children that are held in bondage. They are also too afraid of the curses by the fetish priests to actually sentence them for enslaving the trokosis. The seized trokosis would also be replaced with other little virgin girls as soon as they are taken.

With the Afrikania Mission advising the fetish priests and shrines, the government officials know that the power they wield is very real, so the question is how can the rights of the trokosis be protected? Who is willing to step in and stop the abuse? Who is not afraid of the "big, bad wolf" or better known as The Afrikania Mission?

I personally feel that the people representing the Afrikania Mission need to be charged to the fullest extent of the law, for not only failing to help their own African women and children to get out from under the bondage of slavery, but for encouraging the enslaving of their own people. They mask their evil deeds under the guise of religion and culture. Instead of assisting the fetish priests in the practice of trokosis, they need to be doing everything in their power to show love and respect, and encourage the release of their enslaved sisters. As well, they need to insist that animals be taken to appease their gods instead of human beings. At one time, animals were given in payment for sin or crime. Why can they not go back to those "roots?"

About three or four hundred years ago, women were given to the war deities of the shrines, as at that time there was a lot of waging war between the neighbouring tribes, and by giving a girl or woman to the shrine, it was hoped to bring good luck in winning the battle. At times I heard it said that if a particular god was very angry, a trokosi would actually be sacrificed in the shrine to appease the angry god. This was supposed to be one of the closely guarded secrets of the shrine. It still happens today on occasion, as I understand, but then again, with such a spirit of fear, who is going to come forward and talk about those things upfront?

A chief of a village we visited, and his adorable little son –
the apple of his eye

A liberated trokosi with her husband and child. Their home
is in the background.

A typical village with the mud homes and thatched roofing

One of the twin
daughters of Alicia (a
liberated trokosi),
selling kenkey beside
the road

The old school building made of thatching.

The new school building that was built with the help of sponsors of International Needs – just opened two weeks ago.

The author's sponsored child Kafui (in the middle holding the bag of goodies) with some school children who walked to Kafui's village

A Mother and son pushing their gathered fire wood home

A potter getting her clay dishes ready for the market

Patience (in the centre) with her oldest sister, and an intriguing gentleman from her village. They are all wearing their funeral clothing

A beautiful mother and her little girl in one of the villages of the Volta Region

This little fellow was having a bath and was terrified when he saw the author come after him with the camera

Two students at the Adidome Training Centre with their gift bags. They were daughters of liberated trokosis and had been born out of rape by the fetish priest

The author's sponsored child Kafui, with her mother and little brother

Chapter 10

The Funeral

January 31st

I *am anticipating traveling home today. I hope I will welcome the snow again after this incredible heat. I miss my home and my family and I don't think that I would go so far from home "alone" again for this amount of time. This has been an experience that I won't ever forget. It has been good.*

I had a case of the "runs" a couple of nights ago, and was hoping that it wouldn't last too long, or that it wasn't too serious. It started with terrible cramps during that day and I "barfed" because of the pain – I was nauseous. That didn't last too long, so I just dismissed it for the rest of the day. Well, that night it attacked again about every fifteen minutes and ran out of me like a tap. I ate Imodium as though they were mints, and I must say that eventually they do work. I was informed that morning that we were going somewhere, so after taking them all night long, I took another one, and then another one a half hour later, and still a third one some time later(for the road). A fourth one followed (just in case). After that, nothing moved – for quite a few days. Thank you Imodium!

I packed my suitcases last night, trying to shift the weight equally in each of the large two pieces of luggage that I brought. The batik fabric weighed a lot, but as a quilter I had to buy them. As well, I had purchased a beautiful clay bowl decorated with beads, that I wanted to make sure did not get broken en route home. I also had my back pack that I thought would be lighter this time around, with most of the batteries and snacks used up. I still had to fit the Baobab tree fruit and the two coconuts in somehow (had I known that the coconuts were already rotten, I would have had more room). Oh, and I had to make room for the loofa sponges too – without breaking them. I didn't want to remove the outer dried skin before getting home.

I figured that I couldn't wear my caprice pants and flip flops on the way home, as I would look a little silly in the snow, so I decided to put on my long black polyester pants and top with a pair of lightweight shoes for the trip. I was thinking about not being wrinkled while I traveled. I carried a light jacket. I had left my winter coat in my car at the airport, so that I would have it on my drive back home from the airport. My plan was to stay in the guest house with the air conditioner on "full speed" until the driver came for me, and then he would put the air conditioner on in the vehicle, so I would be nice and "dry" for the duration of the two hour trip to the airport in Accra. With that plan in place, the driver showed up and we were off to Accra, or so I thought.

We no sooner had gotten into the vehicle (or maybe we were even walking toward it) when Patience informed me that we were going to a funeral along the way, as she was related to some of the people that would be there, and wanted to give her condolences. She politely asked me if that was okay, and I thought, "Why not, it will be another experience to educate me further on the Ewe culture."

Besides, it would have been rather rude to have said that I would rather not go. I was looking forward to it.

It was quite a lengthy drive, but it was cool enough in the vehicle. After an hour or so, we ended up in a town where a whole choir was traipsing across the road in front of us and down the street, with drums and other rhythmic instruments, and they were all singing together – wearing beautiful matching dresses (shirts for the men). It was all quite interesting. Patience said that they were going to a funeral too. I saw several ladies walking together in lovely identical dark coloured African dresses and headscarves. They were part of the funeral too, and they were family so they dressed alike. The closer the members were to the deceased, the darker their fabric was.

We waited for the funeral choir to cross, and then carried on to the next town where Patience had some relatives at the funeral. It was an older woman who passed away, and it had been expected, so it wasn't as sad as if a child had died. Apparently, before we arrived she had already been buried, and now everyone was visiting and eating. It was quite similar to any other funeral in the fact that everyone gave their condolences and moved around visiting with whom they wanted.

There were the traditional greetings again and until that was finished you could not just get up and move on. You had to greet the elders or important ones in the group out of courtesy, and then you could go visit with the next little group gathered under another tree. The same three sentence dialogue that they said at the villages was also said here, and then one could say or ask whatever pleased them.

I was introduced to an awful lot of Ewe people and was welcomed by them all with a royal handshake. I noticed that the men in the circle would shake hands with each other, and as they slid their hand away they would somehow snap their fingers, but it was snapped off of the other person's finger – not just your two fingers – one of yours and one of his. I wanted to learn how to do that handshake, so one of the gentlemen showed me how to do it. It looked easy, but took a bit of practice.

I could take pictures once I got permission. Everyone loved to have their picture taken, but you had to ask first, just to be polite.

All of the men were wrapped in many yards of fabric and it was thrown over one shoulder like the fetish priest, but these wraps were wonderful colours that sucked me in (as I am a quilter, and I am sure I could make several quilts out of one of those lovely wraps). One gentleman sitting in front of me looked fascinating. I was convinced that he must be a chief or some other powerful person of authority. He was a large man – maybe 350 pounds and he intrigued me, so I asked Patience if I could take his photo. He had no problem with that. I believe that he was from the village where Patience grew up, so I took a photo of the large man and of Patience and her oldest sister. He seemed like a very jolly, kind man. I didn't catch his name though. Actually, I just couldn't remember it.

The women were all very beautifully dressed in the most amazing African outfits and headscarves. The babies were so sweet. One little fellow was following me, so I picked him up and said that I was taking him home with me. He was ready to go! Most of the little kids were afraid of me pointing my camera at them, but not this little guy. We visited for some time and then Patience thought we would have to leave to get to Accra in time for my flight since I wanted to shop a bit first. I had a nice time and was glad that we went there. I just about died with the heat (or thought I would) with those long black polyester pants and shirt. My hair was a mass of curls and fuzz by that time as it was wringing wet, but no different than the rest of my body. I was gathering sweat and dirt on my clean clothes and realized that my dream of being able to stay "fresh" all the way to the airport was now just a myth. I was going to stink all the way home for the next forty eight hours and there was nothing I, or anyone else (sitting beside me) would be able to do about it – so there.

We were off and I smelled some great beef and rice coming from the front seat of the vehicle. I hadn't had beef in two weeks or more. It smelled wonderful! Patience was eating it, but advised me not to touch it since the "curse of the runs" could pop up again at any time. It was part of the funeral food. With that she generously passed me some fried plantain that she had prepared for me in advance, especially for the trip. I didn't think I could eat plantain again, fried, steamed or baked (because I am spoiled and already ate it for two weeks) and so I passed it on to her sister who happily ate away. I dipped into it a little bit to be polite.

The sister of Patience had to be dropped off to catch another ride to her village, so we did that about forty km. from Accra and said, "Goodbye." We were anxious to get to Accra to have a nice restaurant meal - my treat, however I just had to get some plain wooden spoons for my friend Ruth and I thought they would make good gifts for others as well, but these had to be purchased where the locals shopped, not at the fancy art centre.

We went to the art centre first and I ended up finding some hand carved salad spoons with giraffe and lion handles, so I bought two sets. We went everywhere looking for plain wooden spoons to no avail. There were signs on the walls by the art centre warning people not to urinate on those walls. It seemed as though all the men would urinate wherever they wished, whenever nature called without drawing too much attention to themselves. Some of the little boys just whipped it out on any main street and relieved themselves. It was natural, I guess.

The vendors surrounded the car again, after I thought that I had successfully escaped back into the comfort of the air conditioning. They were tapping on the windows with their little hand carved wooden elephants, and banging the drums that they were trying to sell. I ended up buying a beautiful drum which I somehow managed to cram into an already full suitcase. I finally got out of the vehicle back into the heat and followed Patience for her purchase, which was quickly made. She knew exactly what she wanted and where to buy it. We finally managed to find the place where local vendors bought and sold. It was a challenging few streets for me, and I wasn't even driving!

On every street you could see vendors set up all over the sides of the roads, and I mean all over. They weren't just set up by the edge. There was barely room enough for one vehicle to pass by in some spots. There were big letters on the walls saying, "No hawking by law," but that didn't stop anyone. They needed to make a living somehow and this is the way all the locals shop. There were washers and dryers by the road (I don't think too many people had electricity or power for that, but…) some vendors had furniture by the roads –dozens of sets of identical sofas. One obviously wealthy vendor had dozens of bicycles in an open area, and yet another sold loaves of bread right beside a greasy motorcycle repair place. They were repairing the motorcycles outdoors, right beside the road.

The fruit looked and tasted wonderfully and was stacked up very decoratively. They took a lot of pride in what they did, and it showed. Just because they didn't sell the "American" way, didn't mean that it was any less a business for them. Because of the fact that there is no public assistance, even for the handicapped, they know that they have to work hard, in order to survive and have a reasonably good life. They work their way up in business, starting with something such as gum or candy, and trade up each time they can, so eventually they are selling African art or jewellery to the passing motorists. They have the hope of getting their own space or stand beside the road where buyers will go to them.

I asked Patience if there was a food bank in Accra, and she said that there wasn't a food bank anywhere in Ghana. I mentioned that it would probably be empty in a matter of an hour if there was one, and Patience said, "Oh, no! Only the very destitute, blind or extremely handicapped would take food from a food bank, as they had a lot of pride in being vendors and making a living."

When Patience finally found someone who had some wooden spoons for sale we stopped and managed to cross the road – literally taking our own lives into our hands with the oncoming traffic. We bought all that the vendor had – maybe a dozen or so. The vendor's friend made sure that it was safe for me to cross the road again. The spoons were well made and heavy. Patience asked me to mail some gifts to a friend of hers in Canada as the cost of sending it from Ghana was too much. I happily obliged. It was the least I could do for all of her hospitality to me in the last two weeks.

With all of our searching for the wooden spoons, etc. it was too late to go for our quiet dinner and still make my *international flight, so I was just quickly dropped off at the airport to get on my flight back home.*

We said our quick goodbyes and hugs, after I got the e-mail address for Patience. I would have liked to have visited with her for a while to relax over dinner, but there just wasn't time. I had a very wonderful experience in Ghana that I would never forget. I would go back in a heartbeat (but not alone) as it was a very safe and friendly place. If I did go back to the Adidome Training Center in Ghana someday, I would bring some toys for the children in the nursery as they had no dolls or trucks, etc. to play with.

I was longing for some protein in my diet, and as soon as I got into Amsterdam on my first stop over, I bought the biggest homemade bun with ham and cheese along with a diet Coke from one of the food stands at the airport and was it ever good! Once I got into Minneapolis nine hours later, I bought a meal from McDonald's and it was equally enjoyable. I remembered thinking about how many times my kids wanted to eat at hamburger "joints" and how I went there just to make them happy, but really wanted some "real" food. Now, I was actually enjoying the everyday, ordinary junk food that all of North America takes for granted. I never thought I would enjoy a Big Mac like I did that day.

How much we have to be thankful for in our country - things that Ghanaians have never even heard of or ever hope to experience. They are such a thankful, hard-working and happy people – with exception of the enslaved trokosis – and yet they have so little. They are filled with hope for the future. We as North Americans have it all, but do not realized how truly blessed we really are.

In ending, I wanted to touch on how I ended up traveling to Ghana. Years ago when I was in my late teens, I felt a "calling" to West Africa. I only knew that I would be in the Volta Region and that I would be doing something with English. I had no idea why or when this would happen. It confused me. I tucked it far away into a corner of my mind and I actually forgot about it for many years. A year or so ago, I heard a friend talking about the women and children who were still held as sexual slaves in Ghana and it grabbed my heart in a big way. It was then that I remembered the "calling" from so many years ago. As I further researched the history of International Needs and other groups who were involved in trying to liberating the trokosis, I realized that it had all started many years ago, around the same time that I had felt called to West Africa, so it was all in God's timing. I contacted International Needs and offered to write a book of compiled stories about the liberated trokosis to give them more exposure. I was asked by one of the directors (Bev Dugard) if I wanted to go to Ghana myself as a field worker, to gather my own information regarding the trokosis. I jumped at the chance to be able to give back and do something that I felt would be productive in the hopeful release of even more enslaved women and children.

All of the proceeds of this book will be designated to the release, education and rehabilitation of the enslaved trokosis in West Africa, through International Needs.

I will never forget my experiences in the Republic of Ghana. It was a thrill and a blessing for me to be able to visit with the villagers and children that I met along the way, the staff and students at the Adidome Training Centre, the liberated trokosis who were brave enough and kind enough to allow me to interview them, and to have someone as wonderful and uplifting as Patience for a translator and

209

friend. Thank you and I pray for God's richest blessings for you all.

In closing, I would like to state that it is very expensive to "buy" the liberation of the trokosis. The fetish priests will not give them up without a lot of promises that must be signed for in the contract. Once they have signed, they will keep their word and not enslave any more little virgin girls. The fetish priests and elders demand a high price for their slaves. They want money, livestock, water wells, schools, sponsors, and they want their families to be able to learn trades. The liberation of these women and children comes at a high price. They will not make a deal with the staff of the International Needs organization if they cannot trust them, however International Needs has an excellent reputation with the government officials and the Ewe people of Ghana.

If you would like to be involved with the further liberation, therapy and education of the women and children serving as trokosis, I urge you to please make a donation to International Needs and designate it to the release of the trokosis in West Africa. If you are interested in sponsoring a child in need, I.N. Network can be reached at the following addresses. Thank you and God Bless.

UPDATE: In January 2010 another group of trokosis were liberated from a shrine in Ghana with the help of International Needs.

This was the first liberation ceremony that occurred in several years.

I.N. Network
10432 Chicago Dr. Suite 2
Zeeland, Mi   49464
U.S.A.

I.N. Network
115 First Street, Suite 243
Collingwood, Ont.
L9Y 4W3
Canada

I.N. Network
PO Box 121
Mitcham VIC 3132
Australia

I.N. Network
111b South End,
Croydon, Surrey
CRO 1BJ U.K

I.N. network
PO Box 690 Ds,
Dansoman Estates,
Accra, Ghana, West Africa